31 Days of Faith-Building Moments

A month of scripture-inspired mornings to build your faith and nurture your mental health

Lori R. Miller

Miller Mental Health Services, LLC

Copyright © 2026 by Lori R. Miller

All rights reserved.

No portion of this book may be reproduced in any form without written permission from the publisher or author, except as permitted by U.S. copyright law.

Disclaimer

The content in this book is intended for informational and devotional purposes only and does not constitute professional mental health advice, diagnosis, or treatment. While I am a Licensed Mental Health Counselor, the insights shared here reflect general principles and personal reflections, not individualized clinical guidance. If you are experiencing mental health concerns, please seek support from a qualified mental health professional. In crisis, contact the 988 Suicide and Crisis Lifeline or your local emergency services.

Contents

Dedication	VI
Introduction	VII
The Greatest Love Story Ever Told	XIII
DAY 1: The Love That Won't Quit	1
DAY 2: When God Asks You to Step Into Unknown Territory	8
DAY 3: When Logic Fails and the Sky Is All You Have Left	16
DAY 4: When You're Exhausted from Holding Everything Together	23
DAY 5: Your Calling Is Meant to Be Lived Not Found	30
DAY 6: Choosing Joy When Happiness Runs Out	38
DAY 7: The Proverbs 31 Woman Isn't Your Competition	45
DAY 8: More Than Safe	53
DAY 9: When God Feels a Million Miles Away	61
DAY 10: The Whole Point Was Walking Together	70
DAY 11: You Can't Do This Alone	78

DAY 12: The Rest is in God's Hands	86
DAY 13: God Speaks in Stillness	93
DAY 14: You're Not Going to Blow It	100
DAY 15: When You Can't Feel Him	107
DAY 16: Who Gets Your First Words?	114
DAY 17: When Worry Tries to Do God's Job	121
DAY 18: When Everything That's Broken Gets Fixed	129
DAY 19: When "Good Enough" Costs You God's Best	137
DAY 20: The Difference Between "I Did Wrong" and "I Am Wrong"	145
DAY 21: What Anxiety and Depression Steal From You	153
DAY 22: When God Asks You to Let Go	160
DAY 23: The Work Happens in the Waiting	167
DAY 24: When God Doesn't Explain Himself	174
DAY 25: Stop Living in Tomorrow's Disaster	182
DAY 26: You Can't Earn What You Already Have	190
DAY 27: When God Uses a Donkey	197
DAY 28: Carrying Decisions That Aren't Yours	205
DAY 29: You Can Just Pray Things	213
DAY 30: Standing at the Edge of the Jordan	219
DAY 31: The Day Everything Finally Makes Sense	226
Day 32 and Beyond	233
Small Group Resources	235
A Request	237

About Lori	238
Also by Lori Miller	240
Connect With Lori	242

Dedication

For the ten generations of ministers, martyrs, and believers who came before me — whose steadfast and unshakeable faith in Jesus made mine possible

Introduction

Growing up, no matter how early I got up, my mom was already awake.

I'd find her in the same chair in the living room, Bible open, coffee in her right hand. She'd be there in the quiet before the day started demanding things from her, reading God's word and marking up her Bible like it was the most natural thing in the world.

She told me she'd been getting up early and reading her Bible since she was a little girl.

That little girl had a gift for playing piano that showed up early. She started her training at four years old, and by the time she hit elementary school, she was already a phenom.

Her days were consumed with school and hours of rigorous practice. On top of that, she played the piano at church in the weekend services and midweek, too.

This kind of discipline would've buried most kids her age. But it turns out this wasn't her most disciplined effort.

Before the demands of her education and talent took her full attention for the day, she sat with her Bible. Hearing from the One who created her and knew her heart better than anyone else.

My grandmothers were the same way. I'd find my Gammie in her chair by the window looking out over the lake, glasses in hand, and a simple notebook.

My Memaw would sit in her formal living room in her wingback chair, her Bible in her lap, its pages marked and worn. I remember bookmarks sticking out everywhere like little flags marking territory she'd covered with God.

Memaw would give me my first New Testament Bible when I was about six years old.

The women in my life didn't just talk about wanting to be close to God. They didn't ask God to show Himself to them.

They showed up every morning and put themselves in a place where it could happen. They understood something I'm still grasping at 55: if you want to know God, you have to spend time in His word.

He left us no better way to know Him than this.

How easy is it to let every silly thing in the world crowd that out? The demands start the second you open your eyes.

Kids getting up late for school, bosses texting before you even get to the office, the social media sucking sound that starts the minute you open your phone.

The noise we allow in our lives gets loud fast. Even when we long to develop that kind of discipline, it's too easy to let life encroach on us before we've had time to brush our teeth.

That's where this book comes in.

This book doesn't replace your personal Bible reading. But I hope it spearheads a desire for you to want to know more.

Thirty-one days to think about what God may be calling you to.

Thirty-one days to find stillness before you head into whatever's waiting for you today.

Thirty-one days that lift you up, point you in the right direction, and remind you who you are — and more importantly — whose you are.

So, what exactly is a Faith-Building Moment?

The idea came from my previous book, *31 Days of Mental Health Moments,* which encouraged readers to take a short pause in each day to refocus and prioritize their mental well-being.

But I know there's more to the story than just good mental health. I've learned a lot after two decades in counseling.

Faith and mental health are meant to work together. God created your brain. He understands anxiety, depression, and the weight of stress better than any therapist ever could.

And He's given us scripture and practical tools to help us navigate it.

In my experience, the best faith-building moments come when you go to God first with your challenging emotions or circumstances, then apply in the real world what He shows you.

I can't tell you how many times a certain verse has stood out to me like a neon sign. Later that same day, I'll find an opportunity to use what God showed me.

It's like a perfectly opened door, as if God was saying, "Here you go! I prepared this for you, and I already gave you what you needed this morning to walk through this challenge. You're welcome!"

I find He doesn't often remove the challenge right away because He knows there's growth in there for you in walking through that door.

And He gives us some work to do so we can see just how much we need Him.

This book is designed to help you dedicate a few minutes each day to start scratching the surface of a disciplined daily time with God. This time with Him will help build your faith for all the moments you may encounter throughout the day.

It's not designed to replace your regular Bible study time and prayer each day.

These chapters are designed to enhance what you're already doing and to give you some insight on how to start building healthier habits and patterns in your Christian life.

What You'll Find in Each Chapter

In third grade, I accidentally said a word that rhymed with "witch."

I had a friend whose last name ended in that sound, and I thought it would be funny to take her name through the alphabet. I didn't get very far before I hit the letter "B."

My teacher immediately scolded me. She couldn't believe I, a pastor's daughter, would say such a thing.

Her punishment was writing sentences. I'm a Gen Xer, and when we got in trouble at school, we were told to write the same sentence 100 times on a sheet of paper.

"I will not use bad language in class. I will not use bad language in class. I will not use bad language in class."

I bring that up because I've never forgotten that moment. Writing it down ad nauseam made my transgression real. It held me accountable. And it changed my behavior.

That's why you'll find a lot of writing prompts in this book.

At the end of each chapter, there are two sections:

In This Moment — This is the practical application. You'll be asked to write things down, wrestle with what you've read, and pray. Just like that third-grade punishment taught me something I never forgot, writing down what God is showing you creates lasting change.

Other Moments — These are additional scripture references related to what we talked about in the chapter. Think of them as springboards to take you deeper into the Bible. More opportunities for God to speak to you. More ways to keep building your faith.

Now, let's talk about the Bible translation I'm using.

The B-I-B-L-E! Yes, that's the book for me!

In this book, I chose the New Living Translation (NLT) of the Bible for the scripture verses.

The NLT is perfect for modern readers like you and me because it presents the Bible in clear, conversational language that feels accessible and real. If you're just starting a new Bible habit, the NLT gets straight to the heart of what God's saying.

It's readable without losing the power of the original text. It sounds the way we actually talk, which makes it easier to connect God's truth to your everyday life.

Now, if you're doing deeper Bible study — the kind where you're examining original language, theological nuances, and detailed word-for-word accuracy — you'll want to use a more literal translation like the English Standard Version (ESV) or the New American Standard Bible (NASB). Those are excellent tools for in-depth study and understanding the precise meaning of the original Hebrew and Greek texts.

But for daily devotional reading and practical application, the NLT will serve us nicely.

A quick invitation

These 31 days are just the start. If you want to continue this conversation beyond this book, join me at lorimiller.me/subscribe for more insights on faith, mental health, and living with audacious belief.

But first, the story that changes everything...

Before we jump into Day 1, I need you to understand the story that informs this book and the reason I wrote it.

The Greatest Love Story Ever Told

J esus was the sacrifice for our sins, so that we don't live in eternity apart from Him.

Think about that for a second. Eternity is a long time. Forever separated from the One who created you, who knows you better than you know yourself, who designed you with purpose and intention, and who created you for Him.

That's what was at stake.

God wants nothing more than to live forever with the ones He created in His image. It was the whole point of life in the garden. Imagine daily taking a physical walk with God in the most amazing paradise ever.

Not a metaphorical walk. Not a feeling of His presence during quiet time.

An actual walk in the cool of the day, with the God who spoke the universe into existence.

The free will He allowed in His creations destroyed all that.

Humanity chose its own chains, prompted by a deceiver who tapped into that free will for his own evil purposes.

Do you know this story?

In the beginning, God created Adam and Eve and placed them in a perfect garden. This garden was a paradise where they walked with Him face-to-face in the cool of the day. No separation. No shame. No death. Just pure, unbroken relationship with their Creator.

He gave them one boundary: don't eat from the Tree of Knowledge of Good and Evil. Literally everything else in the garden was theirs for the taking.

But a serpent, who was Satan himself, convinced Eve that God was holding out on them. That they could be like God if they just took what He'd forbidden. So they ate the fruit.

And Adam, who was standing right there next to Eve, followed her cue and chose the same rebellion. In that moment, sin entered the equation and terminated a glorious path for humanity.

Thanks to these two, we've all inherited a spiritual death that puts us constantly on our back foot against God.

You may wonder, what's the big deal about sin?

Sure, people do bad things sometimes. But why does that separate us from God?

Sin isn't just cheating on your spouse or committing heinous crimes. Sin takes that part of us that was so aligned with God as His most precious creation — body, mind, and spirit — and stains it with self-centeredness and rebellion against Him.

Sin isn't just about what we do. It's an inner condition about who we think we are and should be.

Sin is horrific and an affront to a Holy God. Sin and God can't be together.

In the same way light and darkness can't occupy the same space, holiness and sin can't coexist. It's not that God won't allow it, it's that He can't. His very nature makes it impossible.

The larger problem was that if Adam and Eve had stayed in the garden, continuing to eat from the Tree of Life in this new sinful state, they would have lived physically forever.

But they would have been eternally separated from God. There would have been no way back. Imagine what it would feel like to be cut off from the ones you love most for all time.

Cut off permanently, with no hope of ever seeing them again, hearing their voice, or feeling their presence.

That's what sin did. It severed a connection that was never supposed to be broken.

So God had to remove them from the garden so they could physically die and officially terminate that path.

This way, with eternal separation no longer guaranteed, He could provide a sacrifice to right the ship.

It sounds harsh until you realize what God was actually doing.

He was protecting the possibility of redemption. Physical death became the doorway to eternal life instead of the prison sentence of eternal separation.

He offered the most precious thing He had, His only Son, to pay that whole price with a death none of us can really imagine.

Not a symbolic gesture or a metaphor for how much He cares.

An actual, brutal, horrifying death that satisfied the requirement for sin to be paid for.

In that moment, when Jesus died on a cross on a hill in Calvary, the deepest and most entrenched evil turned all its forces on Him.

And He took it, bruised and bloodied, so we wouldn't have to.

Every bit of darkness, every ounce of hatred, every consequence of every sin that had ever been committed or ever would be committed.

All of it landed on Jesus in those final hours. He wiped the slate clean so you and I could walk free and look forward to eternity with Him.

The wild thing is, there's nothing we can do to earn it, it's free.

And we certainly don't deserve it, but all we have to do to get it is to ask for it.

That's it. We don't have to perform in any kind of way, clean ourselves up first, or prove ourselves worthy of it. We don't have to perform a ritual to have access to it.

We just have to ask.

The sacrifices we do make are to daily lay down our own flesh.

Our flesh is that part of us that still wants to point toward that rebellion. We accept Jesus' sacrifice for us, but our carnal desires, if you will, still try to take center stage and place us above God. It's like the rattles of sin still floating around trying to deceive us all over again. We have to sacrifice our own desires and the temptation for rebellion every day to keep that in check.

We like to think we would've done better than Adam and Eve because we're so enlightened. That we would've seen sin for what it was and wouldn't have fallen for the lie.

But every day we make the same choice Adam and Eve made. We believe we know better than God.

Our flesh is weak and always points towards death.

Sacrificing these desires seems impossible at times, and persistent forces outside of us work hard to convince us that our flesh will be what saves us.

The culture around us screams that following your heart and your desires is the path to freedom. That denying yourself anything is oppressive and unhealthy.

But look where following our flesh got Adam and Eve. Look where it gets us every single time.

Our flesh wars against God.

This is why the struggle feels so hard.

But this is the example Jesus sets for us.

If He can lay down his life for all of humanity, then surely we can try to do the same with the things in our lives that trip us up.

In light of His sacrifice, it doesn't feel like too much to ask.

When you really sit with what He did — what He gave up, what He endured, what He rescued you from — suddenly saying no to that thing you know isn't good for you doesn't seem quite so impossible.

And if we can sit even more deeply with how terrible sin truly is, we'll be horrified at the thought of it in light of what He did for us.

The best part is that His sacrifice removes the horrific stain of sin so that we can be in relationship with God again, without limitations or detailed rituals to cleanse ourselves first.

No more wondering if you've done enough. No more anxiety about whether you've measured up. No more performing to try to earn your way back to Him.

The way is open, and the path is clear. Because He cleared it.

We still physically die. But because He rose from the dead and ascended to heaven, if we choose, with our free will, we can spend eternity with Him.

The same free will that got us into this mess in the first place is now the tool God uses to invite us into relationship with Him.

He won't force you. He won't override your choice.

But He's made the way possible.

Jesus didn't come to judge, condemn, or even to set an example.

He came to rescue us from a path we put ourselves on.

Something He didn't have to do, but He desperately wanted to do.

Because He loves you that much.

That's why this is the greatest love story ever told.

DAY 1: The Love That Won't Quit

"Let your unfailing love surround us, Lord, for our hope is in you alone."

— *Psalm 33:22*

Have you ever had that friend you kind of hold your breath around, wondering if they'll actually show up when you need them?

Maybe they show up the first time. Even the second.

But somewhere around the third or fourth time you need them, the excuses start rolling in.

Work got crazy. Life is super complicated. They've got a lot of stuff to deal with.

And you're left wondering if you were ever really high enough on their priority list to matter.

If you've had a friend like that, then I have good news for you.

That's not how God's love works.

The Hebrew Word That Changes Everything

The word for "unfailing love" in this verse is *hesed*.

It's one of those words that doesn't translate cleanly into English because it carries so much weight.

Hesed isn't just a warm feeling God has about you when you're behaving yourself.

It's covenant, committed love. The kind of love that signs on the dotted line and says, "I'm in this no matter what comes."

When the Israelites used this word, they understood they were talking about an obligation. But it was the best kind of obligation.

The kind that says we're bound together, and nothing's going to undo that.

God won't leave because He's frustrated with you. He won't bail because you're not getting it right fast enough.

He won't find something — or someone — better and move on.

What Steadfast Actually Looks Like

When I look back over my life, I can see all the places God's hand was leading me. Especially through the seasons when I had no idea where I was going.

- When the next right step wasn't clear at all.//
- When I'd made mistakes I wasn't sure I could come back from.
- When I felt like I'd disqualified myself from anything good God might have had planned.

I want to be in control. I want to know the plan, see the next five steps, and have a backup plan for the backup plan. If I were God, I'd be pretty frustrated with me.

But He never walked away.

That's what steadfast love does. It shows up in the uncertainty and stays when things get out of control. It doesn't demand you have it all together first.

It meets you right where you are and says, "We're doing this together."

You're Surrounded, Not Stranded

We picture God as above us, seeing all of us, knowing everything happening at the same time. True, but His love isn't where we can't access it.

His love isn't hovering somewhere overhead where you have to perform well enough to reach it.

It's not conditionally offered based on whether you finally get your act together.

It surrounds you, and completely closes you in on every side.

Psalm 139:5 says, *"You go before me and follow me. You place your hand of blessing on my head."*

He's in front of you. Behind you. Beside you. Over you. All the prepositions.

There's nowhere you can go that His love doesn't reach, and no mistake you can make that puts you outside the boundary of *hesed*.

Hope Doesn't Depend on Your Circumstances

We trip ourselves up by trying to conjure up hope like it's a feeling.

But God's hope doesn't depend on anything you do or your circumstances lining up perfectly.

God's hope isn't about your ability to figure this out on your own.

You can't create hope. You have to believe your hope is in the One who's already committed to seeing you through.

Nothing Can Separate You

Romans 8:38 says, *"And I am convinced that nothing can ever separate us from God's love. Neither death nor life, neither angels nor demons, neither our fears for today nor our worries about tomorrow—not even the powers of hell can separate us from God's love."*

You can't do anything to separate yourself from the committed love God has for you. Your past, your mistakes, your failures, and your doubts don't disqualify you from His love.

Maybe you're reading this right now wondering if God could really love someone like you.

Let me help you out. He does. And He won't stop.

Because *hesed* isn't based on you. It's based on Him, and He doesn't change His mind.

This Is Where Your Hope Lives

So when you don't know what's next, when you've messed up again, or when you're wondering if God's finally had enough of you, remember this:

You're surrounded, not stranded. His love isn't going anywhere.

And your hope is not in whether you can hold it together.

It's in the One who's already committed to never letting you go.

***

IN THIS MOMENT

1. **Write down one example of conditional love you experienced.** Name the person and the specific condition they attached to their love. How did that change how you showed up in that relationship?

2. **List three specific ways God has shown steadfast love to you.** What has He done that proved He wasn't going anywhere? Write them down. Be specific with dates, situations, or circumstances, if you can remember them.

3. **Set a phone reminder or alarm** labeled "God's love won't quit" to appear at least twice today. When it goes off, stop

what you're doing and say it out loud: "God's love for me won't quit."

4. **Write this same sentence on a sticky note:** "God's love for me won't quit." Put it somewhere you'll see it multiple times today: your bathroom mirror, your car dashboard, your laptop, or your phone lock screen.

***

OTHER MOMENTS

The faithful love of the Lord never ends! His mercies never cease. Great is his faithfulness; his mercies begin afresh each morning.

Lamentations 3:22-23

Give thanks to the Lord, for he is good! His faithful love endures forever.

Psalm 136:1

Such love has no fear, because perfect love expels all fear. If we are afraid, it is for fear of punishment, and this shows that we have not fully experienced his perfect love.

> 1 John 4:18

Long ago the Lord said to Israel: "I have loved you, my people, with an everlasting love. With unfailing love I have drawn you to myself."

> Jeremiah 31:3

DAY 2: When God Asks You to Step Into Unknown Territory

"This is my command—be strong and courageous! Do not be afraid or discouraged. For the Lord your God is with you wherever you go."

—Joshua 1:9

You know that feeling when you're standing at the edge of something new and your brain is running through every possible worst-case scenario?

The new job that could either launch your career or expose how little you actually know.

The move to a new city where you don't know a soul.

The relationship conversation you've been avoiding because once you say it out loud, there's no taking it back.

The big ask to do something bold might feel like too much. And you're not sure you're the right person for it anyway.

First Project Out of the Gate

Joshua's first assignment after taking over from Moses wasn't exactly a warm-up lap.

His task was to lead an entire nation into the land God promised them. After 40 years of wandering in the wilderness, the time they all had heard about for a generation was about to happen.

That's pretty exciting to think about. But there was a pretty big obstacle.

The Canaanites who currently lived there weren't exactly known for rolling out the welcome wagon for newcomers.

If you were Joshua, how would you feel right now? No pressure.

As he's standing at the edge of the Jordan River, I'm guessing his heart and mind are racing just a bit. How's this supposed to work with the new guy in charge?

There's no personal branding guidebook to help him step out of Moses' shadow. How would you like to follow the guy who parted the Red Sea and talked to God face to face?

But God doesn't give Joshua a pep talk about being inspired by Moses, believing in himself or finding his inner strength.

He simply tells him in direct fashion where real courage comes from.

Two Simple Line Items

God's reassurance to Joshua centers around two things:

    1. Following God's commands, and

    2. Relying on His presence.

Obedience and trust, two things that take the working parts of the situation handily out of Joshua's hands. If Joshua had control issues, this is probably where they would have shown up.

God didn't give Joshua a ten-step strategic plan with fallbacks and redundancies. And He didn't administer a personality assessment to see if Joshua had what it took to deliver.

God's message was just: Do what I say, and know that I'm with you.

When you're facing something that feels too big, it's easy to think God's asking you to muster up bravery from somewhere deep inside yourself. Like courage is something you either have or you don't.

But courage doesn't come from within.

It comes from the nearness of the God who steadies you, leads you, and keeps you.

My Fortune 100 Freakout

I learned about courage when I traded my sweatpants for a cubicle at a Fortune 100 company.

I'd been running my own web design business from home, working in whatever I wanted to wear, making my own hours while my toddler napped. It was comfortable and safe. I was in my element.

But my husband and I wanted to move back to Florida to be closer to my parents. Florida was more expensive so that meant I needed a real job with a steady paycheck.

I somehow landed a position at a Fortune 100 company that was way better than I expected to get.

Suddenly I was sitting in conference rooms with senior leadership, managing multiple projects at once, wearing for-real business clothes, and wondering what on earth I'd gotten myself into. It was overwhelming right out of the gate.

Building a digital empire at home didn't have the prestige then that it does now. I felt like I'd somehow snuck past security and any minute someone would figure out I didn't belong there.

The projects kept piling up. And I had no idea how to manage them all at once.

I remember slipping into a bookstore after work one day and making my way to the business section. To my absolute delight, I found a copy of *Project Management for Dummies*. Just a few days in, and I was already hitting the *Dummies* shelf.

I was terrified, but I knew if He gave me this job, He'd give me what I needed to do it.

Philippians 4:13 says, *"For I can do everything through Christ, who gives me strength."*

If I keep my eyes on Him, I'll have what I need because He would be with me.

I learned more at that job than I have at any other position since. The exposure, the skills, the confidence to produce good work — all of it came from stepping into something I had no business feeling qualified for and watching God provide exactly what I needed.

It wasn't a Red Sea moment where the path suddenly appeared. That would've been nice, especially before I spent money on an expensive book.

But it did come with each day, and each project, and each meeting. That's how God's presence works when you step into unknown territory.

When Therapy Scares the Therapist

When I sat with my first therapy client all on my own, I remember hoping some kind of Red Sea would part for me. Within the wall of water on both sides would be instructions on how exactly to do therapy. That would've been so great.

It's equal parts humbling and terrifying to work with clients on your own for the first time. It creates an existential crisis where all the book smarts and bravado you had about being able to help people goes right out the door when they ask you for the first time, "What do you think I should do?"

It was hard for me not to say, "How should I know?"

My first client was weighing a heavy decision. She had already shed many tears, and needed some help sorting out all her options. Her decision would affect her for the rest of her life.

I remember God slowing me down in my freakout moment, and saying so quietly inside my mind, "I brought her to you. I'll give you what you need to help her."

I'd love to tell you a warm feeling washed over me, but I'd be lying. I still felt like Jell-O on the inside, but I know God's character. He doesn't lie to me. If He says He's going to give me what I need, He will.

That was my cue to open my mouth and say the next thing God had for my client.

I came back to what I'd learned in that Fortune 100 conference room: *I can do everything through Christ, who gives me strength.* Even when I'm terrified.

You're Not Leading Alone

Maybe you feel like God's ask in this season is too much for you to handle.

Or that your best skills are in the shadows, not leading at the edge of promise.

Maybe you're not the charismatic leader, the natural-born speaker, or the person everyone gravitates toward.

Or maybe you think you have no idea what you're doing.

But God isn't just asking you to suck it up and be brave. He's backing it up by promising to be right there with you.

Every step, every decision, every moment when you have no idea what you're doing.

Whatever new land or tough decision you're facing, know that God will walk with you no matter where it leads.

He's never once left me stranded, and He will never leave you hanging.

So be strong and courageous and trust Him with that first step.

***

IN THIS MOMENT

1. **Write out the specific thing you're standing at the edge of right now.** Be concrete. What decision, conversation, or step is God asking you to take? Write it as one clear sentence.

2. **List what scares you about it.** Name 3-5 specific fears. Stay away from ambiguous, vague statements. Let your mind wander to some actual outcomes you're afraid of. Write them down.

3. **Read Joshua 1:9 out loud three times**, inserting your own name: "This is my command — be strong and courageous, [your name]! Do not be afraid or discouraged. For the Lord your God is with you wherever you go."

4. **Tell one person this week:** "I'm stepping into [specific thing] and I'm scared, but I'm doing it anyway because I believe God is with me." Text them, call them, or tell them in person. If you're really serious, post it to your social media channels. I did this in writing this book, and it gave me courage to stay accountable.

***

OTHER MOMENTS

So be strong and courageous! Do not be afraid and do not panic before them. For the Lord your God will personally go ahead of you. He will neither fail you nor abandon you.

Deuteronomy 31:6

Even when I walk through the darkest valley, I will not be afraid, for you are close beside me. Your rod and your staff protect and comfort me.

Psalm 23:4

Don't be afraid, for I am with you. Don't be discouraged, for I am your God. I will strengthen you and help you. I will hold you up with my victorious right hand.

Isaiah 41:10

DAY 3: When Logic Fails and the Sky Is All You Have Left

"For just as the heavens are higher than the earth, so my ways are higher than your ways and my thoughts higher than your thoughts."

— *Isaiah 55:9*

Have you ever sat outside at night, staring at the stars, your mind racing with all the why's of your situation?

Why did this happen? Why didn't God stop it? Why does it feel like He's a million miles away when you need Him most?

Israel knew that feeling.

Staring at Stars Over Babylon

They're in exile. Everything's gone.

The temple is demolished. Their land is stolen. And Jerusalem is a pile of rubble.

They're living in Babylon now, surrounded by people who worship different gods and live by different rules.

They know their disobedience brought them here. But now what?

How does God possibly get them back to His plan from here? The promises He made about their future — about the Messiah coming through their lineage, about being His people forever — feel impossible now.

Logic says there's no path forward. The temple is gone, the place where God's presence dwelled. Their land is occupied. Their nation is scattered.

How do you fulfill prophecies when everything required to fulfill them has been destroyed?

So they gaze at the stars over Babylon, the only way they can look toward God now.

The heavens feel like the closest they can get to Him.

God's Thoughts Soar Higher

But God's thoughts soared higher than that Babylonian sky.

In Isaiah 53, He'd already planned redemption through the Servant, Jesus, who would suffer to bring healing.

That path was already in the books.

They were asking "How do we get back?" God was already working on "How do I bring them home and fulfill every promise I made?"

God's higher way wasn't abandoning the plan. It was completing it through a path they never could have imagined.

Mercy wasn't just forgiveness. It was the continuation of everything He'd promised, just not the way they expected.

I know what it's like to sit in that place where logic says there's no way forward.

When You Can't See Past Tomorrow

The morning I gave notice at my last corporate job, I was shaky.

Twenty years of decent paychecks and in my late forties. The age when you're supposed to be hitting your stride financially, not starting over in a field that pays, well, not so well.

I had no idea how this would work or how I'd replace that income. I didn't even know if counseling full-time would even sustain me or if the timing was actually right. What would happen if I failed?

There had been organizational changes at work. New leadership and new direction coupled with lots of change.

I wasn't leaving because I hated my job or couldn't handle the changes. I was leaving because the direction things were heading wasn't where God wanted me to go, and I knew it.

From the outside, I was worried it would look like I was bailing or like I couldn't adapt.

And I couldn't figure out how to even start the conversation.

I sat on my porch that morning, trying to settle my nerves before I went in to do this thing that made no logical sense.

That's when the dove landed on my reading chair in the corner.

Well, hello there.

We had doves in the yard all the time, but not under the porch. Certainly not five feet from where I was sitting and settling in like it belonged there.

We sat there for a few minutes just staring at each other. I was afraid to move and scare it. I wondered if it was thinking the same thing.

I couldn't see the full plan. But sitting there watching that dove stare back at me, I knew God could.

Doves are a universal sign of peace, and I took it as God saying, "I've got this. You don't have to figure out the timing or the words. I've got you."

Later that day, my boss came to me. "Can I talk to you for a minute? I want to run some things by you."

The conversation she started opened the door I couldn't figure out how to open myself. I had a great segue to give my notice.

She wasn't happy, but she was gracious. Even congratulatory.

It was better than I could have orchestrated.

From where I sat that morning, leaving looked like a big financial risk. From where God sat, it was right on schedule.

Those twenty years I thought I was building a corporate career were preparing me for exactly this moment. That financial risk led to work that actually matters and guess what? God has helped me get past the financial part, too.

God's ways were higher. I just had to trust Him when I couldn't see past the next step.

You Can't See What He Sees

It may feel like the situation has disqualified you from God's plan. Like the devastation is too complete for anything good to come from it.

But He's already a hundred steps ahead of you.

Through Jesus, He turns exile into home by giving you a path back to Him.

God's thoughts for you are vast and merciful.

Instead of gazing sleeplessly at the ceiling, wondering about all the why's of your situation, look at the stars.

They're evidence of how much more He's thought about this than you have.

The Plan Was Already There

God already has a solid plan. He's way ahead of us.

Through Jesus, He turns tough struggles into something real and good.

Your story's not stuck. It's moving forward. Even when you can't see how.

***

IN THIS MOMENT

1. **Write down your biggest "why" question.** The one that keeps you up at night. Be specific. Try to make the question as specific as possible, not just a general question about the topic.

2. **Go outside tonight and look at the stars for five full**

minutes. Don't rush it. Let the vastness of what you're seeing remind you that God's thoughts are higher and vaster than anything you're imagining right now. Do this every night if you can. It will change you.

3. **Take a photo of the night sky** and save it as your phone background or lock screen for this week. Every time you look at your phone, let it remind you: God's ways are higher.

4. **Journal about one past decision where you couldn't see God's plan at the time.** What made no logical sense then? What can you see now that you couldn't see before? Write down the specific ways His thoughts were higher than yours.

***

OTHER MOMENTS

> How precious are your thoughts about me, O God.
> They cannot be numbered! I can't even count them;
> they outnumber the grains of sand! And when I wake
> up, you are still with me!
>
> Psalm 139:17-18

But he was pierced for our rebellion, crushed for our sins. He was beaten so we could be whole. He was whipped so we could be healed.

Isaiah 53:5

For I know the plans I have for you," says the Lord. "They are plans for good and not for disaster, to give you a future and a hope.

Jeremiah 29:11

So now there is no condemnation for those who belong to Christ Jesus.

Romans 8:1

DAY 4: When You're Exhausted from Holding Everything Together

"You made the moon to mark the seasons, and the sun knows when to set."

— *Psalm 104:19*

How many things are you personally managing today?

Your job. Your family. Your finances. Your health. Your relationships.

The mental load alone is exhausting.

You wake up already running through the list of what needs your attention. You go to bed wondering what you forgot. It feels like your mind never stops running the same worried calculations over and over.

And somewhere in the back of that same mind, there's this nagging feeling that if you stop managing it all, everything will fall apart.

We're So Small

When I lived in South Florida, one of my favorite things to do was to sit by the Atlantic Ocean.

I would take a detour from my commute home from work, and plop down in the sand, business casual clothes and all. It was therapeutic to draw in huge breaths with my toes pushed into the sand, and exhale them out with the tide.

As I sat there with the salty wind blowing through my hair, I couldn't help but feel so tiny. The horizon stretched out endlessly in front of me, and from that viewpoint, the earth felt far beyond anything I could control.

If I turned my gaze down just a bit, I'd see little sandpiper birds chasing the water out to grab a quick worm down in the depths of the sand, and then running quickly from it when the water came back in to lap the shore.

Back and forth, chasing the water, then running away to keep from getting pulled out by it.

Even they can't control the tide. They just work with the rhythm God set.

The Sun Doesn't Need Your Permission

I'm grateful I'm not responsible for the sun setting on time, or the moon rising right on cue. If I were, the earth would fall into calamity in less than five minutes.

The sun set last night without you telling it to. And it'll rise tomorrow whether you're awake to see it or not.

The moon is marking the seasons right now, following the rhythm God set in motion long before you showed up.

None of it requires your input, your effort, or your anxiety. God made creation with built-in mechanisms that just... work.

The tides come in and go out. The birds chase the worms beneath it. The earth rotates. Spring follows winter.

But we act like we're the ones who have to keep everything running.

Designed By God, Not To Be God

We've somehow convinced ourselves that our constant vigilance is what's keeping our own world from spinning off its axis.

That if we let our guard down for even a moment, disaster will strike. But that's not how God designed things to work.

God's so big that He set the rhythm for all of creation, and it obeys Him perfectly.

Every single day. Without fail.

What If You're Not Responsible for Everything?

If God can keep the planets in orbit and the seasons on schedule, maybe — walk with me here — you don't have to carry the weight of making sure everything in your life stays in motion.

Maybe some things are meant to operate on the rhythm God set, not the one you're frantically trying to maintain. Your job is to be faithful with what He's given you, to steward it well, and to do the next right thing.

Above all, your job is to trust Him with the outcomes.

Colossians 1:17 says that *"he holds all creation together."*

That means you can stop white-knuckling your way through life, terrified that one misstep will bring everything crashing down.

Here's what's happening when you live this way.

In counseling, I see this pattern all the time. It's called *hypervigilance*. The belief that if you just stay alert enough, manage carefully enough, and think ahead far enough, you can prevent disaster.

It's exhausting because you're trying to do the impossible. Who can prevent disaster? No one. That's the point.

You're trying to control outcomes you were never meant to control. And the irony is the tighter you grip, the more anxious you become.

This need for constant control is costly. Here's what it does to you:

- You can't rest.

- You can't enjoy what's right in front of you.

- You resent the people and responsibilities you're trying so hard to manage.

- Your body holds the tension in your shoulders, your jaw, your stomach.

You're doing damage trying to prevent damage.

Let Go of What Was Never Yours to Hold

This doesn't mean you check out and stop being responsible. It means you understand the difference between responsibility and control.

You're responsible for showing up, doing your part, and doing the best you can to make wise decisions. You're not responsible for controlling outcomes, managing other people's choices, or preventing every possible negative scenario. That's God's job, not yours.

He's already figured out what you can't see.

You can rest knowing He's managing what's beyond your control.

***

IN THIS MOMENT

1. **Make a list of everything you feel personally responsible for right now.** Work. Family. Health. Finances. Relationships. Write it all down.

2. **Go through that list and mark each item** with either "R" (my responsibility) or "C" (trying to control). Circle every item marked "C." These are what you need to release to God.

3. **Choose one thing you circled and write this sentence:** "I release [specific thing] to God. I'm responsible for [what I can actually control], but the outcome belongs to Him."

4. **Tonight, watch the sunset for at least 10 minutes.** No

phone scrolling. Don't even take a picture of it. Just watch it happen without your help. Let it remind you that some things operate on God's rhythm, not yours.

***

OTHER MOMENTS

He will not let you stumble; the one who watches over you will not slumber. Indeed, he who watches over Israel never slumbers or sleeps.

Psalm 121:3-4

Look at the birds. They don't plant or harvest or store food in barns, for your heavenly Father feeds them. And aren't you far more valuable to him than they are? Can all your worries add a single moment to your life?

Matthew 6:26-27

Be still, and know that I am God! I will be honored by every nation. I will be honored throughout the world.

Psalm 46:10

The Son radiates God's own glory and expresses the very character of God, and he sustains everything by the mighty power of his command. When he had cleansed us from our sins, he sat down in the place of honor at the right hand of the majestic God in heaven.

Hebrews 1:3

DAY 5: Your Calling Is Meant to Be Lived Not Found

"Therefore I, a prisoner for serving the Lord, beg you to lead a life worthy of your calling, for you have been called by God."

— *Ephesians 4:1*

Ever feel like everyone else got the Instagram-worthy story about their life purpose that somehow never made it to your feed?

You see their posts, out there doing big things, making a difference, living their calling in great hair and makeup.

And you're just... doing whatever it is you do over here.

Going to work. Taking care of your family. Trying to keep it all together.

Meanwhile, that little voice inside you wonders when God's going to reveal this grand calling you've been hearing about.

The Myth of the Big Reveal

We've created this idea that a calling is a big dramatic moment. A burning bush where God speaks to you and lays out your destiny in crystal-clear detail.

Some massive, unmistakable sign that finally tells you what you're supposed to be doing with your life.

So we wait for it.

And while we're waiting, we miss what's right in front of us.

A Calling Isn't Just for Missionaries

We get it wrong when we think a calling is reserved for pastors, missionaries, and people who work in full-time ministry.

As if God would only call certain people to certain vocations, and the rest of us are just what... existing?

But that's not what Scripture says.

Read Ephesians 4:1 again. *"Therefore I, a prisoner for serving the Lord, beg you to lead a life worthy of your calling, for you have been called by God."*

God calls all of us to reflect His character in our everyday lives.

- In the office

- At home

- In the carpool line

- At the grocery store

- In the middle of a difficult conversation with your teenager.

Your calling isn't some far-off thing you have to hunt down and capture. Your calling is simply being faithful where He has placed you right now.

The irony is that when you're faithful in the ordinary, patterns begin to emerge. You start seeing God's design in what looked like random jobs and disconnected experiences. It took me decades to see mine.

Living Life Called

At 18, I had a political editorial published in a large newspaper. It was a spicy take on the Lloyd Bentsen-Dan Quayle debate that I mailed in and checked for obsessively. When it appeared a week later above the fold with a huge headline, I thought my head would explode. What validation!

But I followed other paths that interested me, too. These paths also happened to pay the bills.

I started in web design in the early days of the Internet, helping people leverage technology they didn't understand. That experience moved me into crafting messages for Fortune 100 companies.

I spent twenty years helping companies get their message out so that those who needed it could actually use it. Even though I was in my groove, the stress of the high-performance environments had me wondering if this was my calling. Making other people's words easier to understand.

Along the way, I helped people in ministry find solutions to their spiritual problems. I became a counselor, working with individuals and couples.

It took me until I was almost 50 to see the pattern, and to see my calling.

I'm a Bridge-Builder

No matter what I do, I spot the gap between where someone is and what they need, then I figure out how to close it.

That's what I was doing at 18 when I helped newspaper readers see a different perspective.

That's what I was doing when I helped people understand technology.

That's what I was doing when I translated corporate strategy into clear communication.

That's what I was doing when I helped people in ministry solve problems.

That's what I did as a counselor and now in my writing, helping people recognize their power to create change and find freedom.

All those skills God gave me the opportunity to build in those younger seasons now intersect. The calling I thought I'd left behind has been there the entire time, woven through every vocation.

I wasn't waiting for my calling to show up. And I didn't find my calling. I recognized it.

Finding implies it was lost or hidden. Recognition means it was there all along. I just hadn't named it yet.

You're Already Living It

Maybe you're like I was, looking for the calling when you're already living it. The pattern is there. You just haven't named it yet.

That job you think is just paying the bills may be where God has you right now. The family you're raising is your mission field. The neighbor who drives you crazy is your opportunity to show Christ's love.

You're not in the waiting room when you're living out the mundane, ordinary, sometimes frustrating circumstances of your everyday life. That's you living right in the middle of your calling.

This is why it's so important for you to be faithful in the small things, show up with integrity, and love people well. You point others to Christ through how you live, not just what you say.

What Does Faithfulness Look Like?

- It looks like doing your work with excellence, even when no one's watching.

- It looks like being kind to your difficult coworker instead of joining the gossip in the break room.

- It looks like choosing integrity when cutting corners or blame shifting would be easier.

None of that feels particularly glamorous or Instagram-worthy. But that's where God often does His best work — in the faithful, quiet, everyday moments when you're simply living like you belong to Him.

Stop Waiting, Start Living

If you're waiting for some grand revelation about your purpose before you start really living, you're going to waste a lot of time.

God has already called you. Living worthy of that calling means reflecting His character in whatever you're doing today.

Right where you are, with the people He's already put in front of you. That's your calling.

Now go live that today.

***

IN THIS MOMENT

1. **Look at your calendar for this week.** Write down three "ordinary" obligations that feel mundane or like placeholders: work meetings, carpool, grocery shopping, laundry, whatever fills your days.

2. **For each of those three ordinary moments, write one specific way you can reflect Christ's character.** Example: "During Tuesday's team meeting, I'll encourage someone instead of staying silent." Or "On the way to school, I'll actually listen when my kid talks instead of planning dinner in my head."

3. **Identify one area where you've been waiting for "something bigger" before you engage fully.** Write it down, then cross it out and write: "This IS my calling right now."

4. **Do one of the three actions you wrote in #2 within the next 24 hours.** Don't wait until you feel inspired, and don't make it a thing. Just do it and see what happens.

***

OTHER MOMENTS

> Work willingly at whatever you do, as though you were working for the Lord rather than for people. Remember that the Lord will give you an inheritance as your reward, and that the Master you are serving is Christ.
>
> Colossians 3:23-24

> Each of you should continue to live in whatever situation the Lord has placed you, and remain as you were when God first called you. This is my rule for all the churches.
>
> 1 Corinthians 7:17

No, O people, the Lord has told you what is good, and this is what he requires of you: to do what is right, to love mercy, and to walk humbly with your God.

Micah 6:8

God has given each of you a gift from his great variety of spiritual gifts. Use them well to serve one another.

1 Peter 4:10

DAY 6: Choosing Joy When Happiness Runs Out

"I have told you these things so that you will be filled with my joy. Yes, your joy will overflow!"

—John 15:11

God commands us to have joy.

That feels like one more thing you're failing at, doesn't it? But joy isn't a luxury. It's a promise.

And God doesn't command things without providing the path to get there.

Connected to the Source

In John 15:5, Jesus uses a vineyard to explain how this whole thing works.

"Yes, I am the vine; you are the branches. Those who remain in me, and I in them, will produce much fruit. For apart from me you can do nothing."

The word "remain" means to stay connected continuously, like a branch that can't survive separated from the vine.

Three components make up this metaphor: the vine, the branches, and the gardener.

Jesus is the vine, the source of nourishment. He's got deep roots that go way down. *"I am the true grapevine, and my Father is the gardener." (John 15:1)*

You and I are the branches, where fruit grows.

And God the Father is the gardener, the caretaker who tends the whole operation. He sees what needs pruning and care.

Your job is to remain connected to the source. When you stay attached, you let the nourishment flow from Him into you.

Love Comes First

Galatians 5:22-23 lists the fruit of the Spirit, *"But the Holy Spirit produces this kind of fruit in our lives: love, joy, peace, patience, kindness, goodness, faithfulness, gentleness, and self-control..."*

Do you notice that love is listed first? That's not an accident.

Love is the first fruit. Everything else — including joy — grows out of that love.

This isn't romantic love (eros) or friendship love (phileo) that operates on what you can get in return.

It's God's love (agape). The completely selfless, outward-focused kind that doesn't keep score. The kind that looks at someone else's need and meets it without calculating what you'll get in return.

That's the first fruit God produces in us when we remain in Him. Everything else flows from that.

So if we can remain in Jesus, getting nourishment from His deep roots, and being cared for by the compassionate gardener, the natural result, the fruit, will be love.

We don't have to try hard to show His love to others. Remaining in the vine will produce that love simply because we are tapped into Him as the source.

Joy Is What Happens Next

Most of us get it wrong when we think joy is something we pursue directly.

Joy is a byproduct of love.

1 John 4:8 is clear: *"Anyone who does not love does not know God, because God is love."*

You can't have joy without love. You can't have love without God. And you can't access any of it without remaining in Him.

His joy in you is not conjured up. His joy flows into you because you're remaining in Him, producing the fruit of love, and letting that love flow outward.

When you love others with the love you've been shown, your joy is full.

Pruning Keeps You Remaining

It gets uncomfortable when God starts cutting things away.

You're remaining. You're trying to love people well. And suddenly everything falls apart.

But look at what Jesus says: *"He cuts off every branch of mine that doesn't produce fruit, and he prunes the branches that do bear fruit so they will produce even more." (John 15:2)*

That's God pruning you.

If you're remaining in the vine, He's going to prune. That fruit you're producing is amazing, but it needs to be cut off because it's keeping you from producing something even better.

The gardener's job is daily. If you're breathing, God is pruning you.

When that happens we stop remaining. We try to figure it out in our own strength. We disconnect from the vine because pruning can hurt.

If a branch touches the ground and stays there, it withers. You end up barely hanging on, wondering why joy feels so far away.

The paradox, though, is if you stop remaining, you can't produce the fruit of love. And you don't have access to joy.

Pruning isn't punishment. It's what keeps you remaining and alive and producing fruit.

As a therapist, I see people white-knuckle their way through anxiety and depression, trying to manufacture peace through sheer willpower.

But you can't think your way to joy. And you certainly can't perform your way there.

The only path is remaining connected to the source of life even when everything in you wants to disconnect and figure it out yourself.

That's where nourishment is, and that's where joy becomes real.

What Joy Actually Feels Like

Joy isn't happiness on steroids. It's not Happiness 2.0 or that giddy feeling when everything's going your way.

Joy is contentment. That exhale of "Okay, I can handle this" because you know God's got it.

You've seen people whose lives are objectively difficult, yet they carry this peace that doesn't make logical sense. That's what remaining in the vine produces.

When you bear the fruit of love, you reflect God's love to the world. That's when joy shows up as a byproduct.

You Can Choose Joy Because You Can Choose to Remain

When things threaten to knock you off course, you say, "I don't understand it. But I'm going to keep remaining."

You stay connected, and you keep producing the fruit of love.

Joy is a result of your relationship with Christ. You choose joy by choosing to remain in that relationship.

Remaining isn't passive. It requires intentionality. That's why it feels so hard sometimes.

Pray. Read the Bible. That's how God talks to you. That's how His words remain in you.

Find time to be still. Say, "God, what do You want me to hear?" Then be quiet long enough to listen.

That's where God speaks. That's where you settle back into your role as the branch, not the vine.

So remain there.

***

IN THIS MOMENT

1. **Read John 15:1-12 out loud.** Count how many times Jesus uses the word "remain." Write that number down and circle it. What's He emphasizing?

2. **Write down one specific area where you've been trying to manufacture joy through your own effort.** What are you doing to force it? Now write: "I'm releasing my grip on this and remaining in Christ instead."

3. **Identify one specific person you can show agape love to this week.** This is the kind that costs you something and expects nothing back. Write their name and what you'll do. Then set a reminder on your phone to actually do it.

4. **Spend 10 minutes today in complete stillness.** No music,

books, phone or agenda. Just sit quietly and practice remaining connected to the Vine instead of striving to produce fruit on your own. Journal about the feelings that come up for you.

***

OTHER MOMENTS

Whoever does not love does not know God, because God is love.

1 John 4:8

You will show me the way of life, granting me the joy of your presence and the pleasures of living with you forever.

Psalm 16:11

...Don't be dejected and sad, for the joy of the Lord is your strength!

Nehemiah 8:10

DAY 7: The Proverbs 31 Woman Isn't Your Competition

"She is clothed with strength and dignity, and she laughs without fear of the future."

— Proverbs 31:25

She wakes up early, runs a business, makes her own clothes, feeds the poor, manages servants, invests in real estate, stays up late, never eats the bread of idleness.

Oh, and her husband praises her and her children rise up and call her blessed.

If you've ever read Proverbs 31 and felt like you're failing at life, you're not alone.

Meanwhile, you're just trying to get through the day without yelling at your kids or losing your cool when the TV remote disappears.

The Performance Trap

We turn this scripture passage into a checklist, a standard we'll never meet. We look at this woman and think, "Holy cow, I'm nowhere close."

So we beat ourselves up for not measuring up.

Men, if you're reading this chapter and thinking "This doesn't apply to me," stick with me. The principle here isn't just about women measuring up to an impossible standard.

It's about all of us comparing ourselves to composite pictures of excellence that were never meant to be checklists.

The Great Sock Dilemma

When my son was six or seven, I brought him a basket of clean socks and said, "Fold your socks and put them away."

When I checked later, the basket was empty. Sweet. Then I opened his sock drawer.

He'd just dumped them all in there. No folding. No neat little sock balls like my mother had taught me to make, laying them side by side, folding one over the other into a perfect bundle.

I found him on the floor playing with trains.

"I thought I asked you to fold and put the socks away."

"I did," he said.

"But look, they're all just thrown in here. You didn't fold them."

He looked at me like I was speaking a foreign language.

"Mom. They're all the same kind of sock. Same color. Why would I fold them?"

I stood there holding that drawer open, ready to explain why we fold socks because that's what we DO, and then I actually thought about it.

He was right. On a busy school morning, he'd grab two socks and win every time.

There was no compelling reason for him to fold those socks. This wasn't about teaching him a life skill. This was about me needing everything to look perfect, even when it didn't matter.

I was trying to be the Proverbs 31 woman who does everything with excellence — apparently including sock management.

Holding onto that detail meant I had less energy for things that day that actually mattered.

Sometimes faithfulness means letting go of the folded socks.

A Portrait of Potential

A pastor's wife changed everything for me when she said this:

> ***Proverbs 31 isn't about perfection. It's about potential.***

Each thing this woman does represents what can be done. Proverbs 31 isn't what you must do, or even what you should do.

It's a picture of the many ways someone can use their gifts and abilities.

The point isn't to do all of it. The point is to explore your own potential in the areas God has uniquely wired you for.

She's a Composite, Not a Competitor

This woman is described doing things that would require multiple lifetimes to master.

She's a textile expert, a business owner, a real estate investor, a philanthropist, a wife, a mother, a manager.

That's not one woman. That's a composite picture of excellence.

Thinking of her as the height of perfection is like looking at a gallery of masterpieces and thinking you're supposed to paint all of them yourself.

What's Your One Thing?

Some women are wired for business. Some are gifted with their hands, they create beautiful things. Some have the gift of hospitality. Some are called to serve the poor and marginalized.

Men are supposed to be the provider, the protector, the spiritual leader, the hands-on dad, the servant-hearted husband, the successful professional, and the guy who can fix anything.

Both are pretty tall orders. Proverbs 31 shows us all these possibilities. We can't do them all, but we can find the ones God is calling us to.

She Laughs Without Fear

Look at verse 25 again: *"She is clothed with strength and dignity, and she laughs without fear of the future."*

She laughs.

You know why? Because she knows who she is. She knows what she's good at. And she's not trying to be anyone else.

Strength and dignity aren't about doing everything perfectly or being the benchmark others measure themselves against. They're about doing what you're called to do with confidence in God's provision for you.

Stop Measuring, Start Exploring

What if instead of measuring yourself against impossible composites, you asked: What has God called me to do in this season?

- Maybe you're not called to run a business. Maybe you're called to run toward the people everyone else overlooks.

- Maybe you're not called to buy a field. Maybe you're called to cultivate your children's hearts.

- Maybe you're not called to be the hero in every story. Maybe you're called to be faithful in the one story God wrote for you.

You're Supposed to be You

Clothed with strength and dignity. Laughing without fear of the future. Because you've discovered what God created you to do, and you're doing it with everything you've got.

The specific details of Proverbs 31 may describe a woman, but the heart of it — discovering your God-given potential instead of comparing yourself to impossible standards — is for all of us.

That's the potential Proverbs 31 points to. You, fully alive in the gifts God gave you, serving the people He put in front of you.

That's enough. And you are enough.

***

IN THIS MOMENT

1. **Read Proverbs 31:10-31.** As you read, instead of feeling guilty about what you're not doing, circle or note the things that resonate with your actual gifts and calling.

2. **Make a list of three things you're naturally good at.** These aren't things you think you should be good at. Try to come up with those that come naturally and bring you joy.

3. **Ask yourself:** What season am I in right now? Young kids? Career building? Empty nest? Caring for aging parents? What does faithfulness look like in this season? Try to focus on areas outside of where you think you should be, but the reality of where you are.

4. **Identify one area where you've been comparing your-

self to an impossible standard.** Write down the thoughts you tell yourself about how you think you're doing in this area. Look specifically for the word "should." This is a clue about where your focusing on perfection instead of potential.

5. **Practice laughing.** Seriously. Find something that makes you laugh today. Watch a short video of your favorite comedian. Look at funny videos of your kids or grandkids on your phone. Joy and laughter aren't luxuries. They're signs of someone who knows who they are and whose they are.

***

OTHER MOMENTS

In his grace, God has given us different gifts for doing certain things well. So if God has given you the ability to prophesy, speak out with as much faith as God has given you. If your gift is serving others, serve them well. If you are a teacher, teach well. If your gift is to encourage others, be encouraging. If it is giving, give generously. If God has given you leadership ability, take the responsibility seriously. And if you have a gift for showing kindness to others, do it gladly.

Romans 12:6-8

God has given each of you a gift from his great variety of spiritual gifts. Use them well to serve one another.

1 Peter 4:10

Pay careful attention to your own work, for then you will get the satisfaction of a job well done, and you won't need to compare yourself to anyone else. For we are each responsible for our own conduct.

Galatians 6:4-5

You made all the delicate, inner parts of my body and knit me together in my mother's womb. Thank you for making me so wonderfully complex! Your workmanship is marvelous—how well I know it.

Psalm 139:13-14

DAY 8: More Than Safe

"This I declare about the Lord: He alone is my refuge, my place of safety; he is my God, and I trust him."

— Psalm 91:2

There's a difference between being safe and having a refuge.

Safety says, "I'll keep you from danger."

Refuge says, "Come in here where no one can find you."

When You Need More Than Protection

We talk about God keeping us safe. And He does. But sometimes you need to get out of sight completely after you've been fighting for a while.

You need cover or concealment, a place where the storm can't touch you and your enemies can't see you.

You need a refuge.

The Cave at En Gedi

When David wrote Psalm 91, he wasn't king yet, sitting in a palace surrounded by guards. He was running for his life.

Samuel had already anointed him as the next king of Israel. God Himself had chosen David, and Samuel declared it publicly.

Saul knew God had rejected him as king and chosen David instead. So David spent years hiding in caves, fleeing from Saul, living like a fugitive.

God's promise was real, and His anointing surely was real. But the threat from Saul was just as real.

There's a moment in 1 Samuel 24 that shows you exactly what David's refuge looks like.

David and his men are hiding deep in a cave at En Gedi. Saul is hunting him with 3,000 men. The entire army is searching for David to kill him.

And then Saul walks into the exact cave where David is hiding.

Saul needs to relieve himself, so he steps into the cave for privacy. You can only imagine how David's eyes must have widened.

David is concealed in the darkness at the back of the cave. Saul is standing at the entrance, completely vulnerable, and unaware that the very one he sought was right next to him.

David's men whisper, "This is it! God has delivered your enemy into your hands!"

But David doesn't move. He simply cuts off a corner of Saul's robe to prove he was there, but he doesn't harm him.

Later, after Saul leaves, David calls out from a distance and shows him the piece of robe. Saul realizes how close he came to death and how completely God had hidden David.

God didn't remove the threat. He concealed David while the threat walked right past him.

Being chosen by God doesn't exempt you from needing a place to hide. Even when you're walking in your calling, you still need refuge.

Refuge doesn't remove the threat. It removes you from the threat's reach.

The Hebrew word for refuge in Psalm 91 is *machaseh*, a shelter, a hiding place. God doesn't just protect you. He conceals you.

What a Refuge Does

A refuge does three things that simple safety doesn't:

1. A refuge shields you from the elements, not just the enemy

The pressure of constant attack makes you feel open and exposed, and hijacks your focus.

I see people who've been in fight-or-flight mode so long they've forgotten what it feels like to not be on high alert. Their nervous systems are stuck in overdrive waiting for the next threat on the horizon.

They can't rest. Their focus is shot. And they feel like they're always making decisions out of exhaustion and panic.

One of the first things I teach them is grounding techniques. Everything we're worried about is in the future, and we tend to live there when we're under pressure.

Grounding brings your mind and body back to the present moment by tapping into your senses. What do you see, hear, and feel right now that you can focus on? This redirects your mind back to where your body actually is.

This is especially important when working with clients dealing with trauma. Reliving traumatic experiences brings your body right back to that event. You have to learn how to ground yourself in the present where you're currently safe.

God's refuge provides this kind of safety, a place where your nervous system can finally stand down.

2. It gives you time to recover.

Refuges aren't permanent addresses. You're just passing through. They're places you go to recover so you can re-engage.

You don't set up camp and stay in the refuge from now on. That will keep you from realizing the purpose and plans God has for you. And it will keep God from being able to show you His power when coming up against challenges.

David didn't live the cave life forever. But he needed the cave to survive long enough to fight another day.

God's refuge isn't about hiding from life. It's about having a place to recover so you can return to life without being destroyed by it.

3. It allows you to observe from a safe place.

When I lived on the East Coast of Florida, I'd visit the House of Refuge at Gilbert's Bar. It's Martin County's oldest structure, and Florida's last remaining life-saving station.

Built in 1876, it stood on the beach as a literal refuge for shipwrecked sailors. Keepers and their families lived there, walking the shores after storms to rescue anyone who'd washed up on that treacherous coastline.

The House sat right on the edge of the ocean, exposed to every hurricane and storm that came through. But it was built to withstand the elements. It was a place where survivors could watch the storm that nearly killed them from a position of safety.

From inside those walls, shipwrecked sailors could see the wreckage of their ship, assess what was lost, and figure out what they could do next. The refuge gave them a vantage point to be still and process what had happened without being destroyed by it.

That's what God's refuge does for you.

What It Looks Like to Hide in God

So how do you actually take refuge in God when He's not a physical cave?

You get still.

Refuges require stillness. Pacing and worrying defeats the purpose. Psalm 46:10 says, *"Be still, and know that I am God!..."*

You bring Him what's hunting you. David didn't just sit in the cave hoping Saul would leave. He brought his fear, his exhaustion, and his impossible situation directly to God. So many of the Psalms were David doing exactly this.

Name what you're running from. Say it out loud to God.

- "I'm afraid of failing."

- "I'm ashamed of what I did."

- "I can't handle this pressure anymore."

When you speak it to Him, you're no longer carrying it alone.

Open your Bible, turn to Psalms, pick any of them, and let God's words replace the lies circling in your head.

Sit in silence and listen. You don't run in to a refuge, catch your breath for 30 seconds, and run back out. Stay long enough to let the panic subside and to remember you're not alone.

Let yourself feel settled, knowing you're not alone, you're not forgotten, and He's got you.

Bring Him the threat and let His presence conceal you.

***

IN THIS MOMENT

1. **Identify what you're running from right now.** Notice what makes your body tense up or what thoughts keep you awake at night. Is it fear? Shame? Anxiety? Fierce pressure? Put a name on it and label it.

2. **Find a physical place where you can be still for 20 minutes.** Narrate your immediate environment out loud as if you're describing it to someone who can't see it. "I'm sitting in a gray chair. There's a window to my left. I can see a tree outside..." Describe what you see, what you hear, what you're touching. Speaking out loud forces you into the present moment.

3. **Bring what you named in #1 to God in prayer.** Don't clean it up or make it sound churchy or spiritual. Just tell Him: "I'm terrified. I'm exhausted. I can't do this." Then read Psalm 91. Let God's promises about refuge replace the fear circling in your head.

4. **End with this declaration:** "He alone is my refuge." Make it a statement of fact about where you're choosing to stay.

***

OTHER MOMENTS

> God is our refuge and strength, always ready to help in times of trouble.
>
> Psalm 46:1

My victory and honor come from God alone. He is my refuge, a rock where no enemy can reach me. O my people, trust in him at all times. Pour out your heart to him, for God is our refuge.

> Psalm 62:7-8

The name of the Lord is a strong fortress; the godly run to him and are safe.

> Proverbs 18:10

My God is my rock, in whom I find protection. He is my shield, the power that saves me, and my place of safety. He is my refuge, my savior, the one who saves me from violence.

> 2 Samuel 22:3

DAY 9: When God Feels a Million Miles Away

"Is anyone thirsty? Come and drink.."

— Isaiah 55:1

Israel is in exile. Babylon has destroyed everything. The Israelites' identity as God's people is shattered. They've been relocated and assimilated. Their covenant with God feels cut off, like ancient history.

What now?

If you've ever felt spiritually dry, like God is distant and you can't find your way back, you know exactly how they felt.

Rock Bottom with No Ladder

This is Israel's lowest point. The sin that separated them from God has built a wall so high they can't see over it. Everything that connected them to Him is gone.

No temple to worship in. No land to call home. No kingdom to belong to.

They're living in Babylonian culture now, trying not to forget who they used to be.

The spiritual dryness is suffocating. They're thirsty for God, desperate for Him even.

But after everything they've done, after the way they broke the covenant, how could He possibly still want them?

An Unexpected Invitation

And that's when God speaks. Not with condemnation or an "A-ha! I told you so."

But with an invitation.

Another version of Isaiah 55:1 says, *"Come, all you who are thirsty, come to the waters..."*

Come is present tense. Right now. All you who are thirsty *right now*, come to the waters.

From the middle of their spiritual desert, from the depths of their desperation, God extends grace.

Free water for your extreme thirst. He hasn't forgotten you.

Spiritual Dehydration Is More About Source Than Sin

My Christian clients express a particular kind of frustration. They are grateful for what Jesus did on the cross for them. But they still describe a particular kind of emptiness that no achievement, relationship, or distraction seems to fill.

They've tried therapy, self-help books, new careers, different relationships, more discipline, less discipline.

And they're still thirsty.

Spiritual thirst shows up in ways all too familiar to many of us:

- **Chronic dissatisfaction.** Nothing feels like enough. No accomplishment seems to satisfy for long.

- **Restlessness.** You're constantly looking for the next thing, hoping this will be what finally settles you and get you where you want to go.

- **Performance anxiety.** The relentless drive to prove with your skills and gifts that you're worthy and valuable enough.

- **Emotional numbness.** Going through the motions and doing all the things, but feeling disconnected from your own life.

Sometimes this is clinical depression or *anhedonia,* the inability to feel pleasure. But sometimes it's not a diagnosis.

Sometimes it's profound spiritual dehydration that has set in.

I need you to hear this: I'm not saying you're not praying enough or that you're too much in sin. None of us can earn God's grace through our efforts. We're all dependent on Jesus for our righteousness."

But I am saying that anything apart from what Jesus offers is like trying to hydrate with salt water.

You're reaching for things that promise relief but ironically, leave you thirstier than before.

Success. Approval. Control. Comfort. None of it can do what only God can do.

The Choice Point

I hang my psychological theory hat largely on Acceptance and Commitment Therapy (ACT). In ACT, we use something called the Choice Point Model.

Imagine you're standing at the center of two arrows.

One arrow points toward what you value, what matters most to you, what you actually want your life to be about.

The other arrow points away from it, toward avoidance, distraction, short-term relief that doesn't solve anything.

At the intersection is the Choice Point, the moment you decide which direction to move. Every single day, in a million different situations, you're standing at that choice point.

You can take committed action toward what you value, which as a Christian means moving toward God, toward His presence, toward the life He's calling you to.

Or you can move away from it, choosing the easier, more comfortable path that doesn't require trust or surrender.

It sounds easy enough. But moving toward what you value requires letting go of what's not serving you, and more importantly, the things you're using to prove your worth apart from God.

And that's where most of us get stuck.

You Can't Drink While You're Carrying

Philippians 4:6 says, *"Don't worry about anything; instead, pray about everything. Tell God what you need, and thank him for all he has done."*

That's not "pray it away and hope it disappears." It's a command with an action.

Don't be anxious — instead, pray.

The action is giving your anxiety, fear, worry, sadness, restlessness, and disillusionment to God. Picture yourself laying it at the foot of the cross, and not picking it back up.

But it's hard to do that if we're not drinking from the well each day.

People ask me all the time, "Why can't God just take away my anxiety, depression, emptiness, and restlessness?"

And when I ask, "Are you reading your Bible, praying, sitting in silence to hear Him?" the answer is often no. Or it's "I tried that for a week and nothing changed."

They're standing at the choice point, holding onto what's making them thirsty and trying to drink from a broken straw, asking God to make them feel better while they keep doing the same thing.

You don't drink water the one time and never need to drink again. You have to drink consistently every day.

God wants to show you how to grow through what you're facing. But He can't if you won't come to the well.

What If You've Been Coming to the Well and Still Struggling?

Maybe this is you:

"I'm reading my Bible every day. I'm praying. I'm doing everything I'm supposed to do. Why do I still feel anxious? Why am I still depressed? Why hasn't God fixed this?"

I get it. It's frustrating to feel like you're doing everything right and still struggling.

My best answer is that coming to the well isn't a transaction. It's a relationship.

Sometimes God uses the discipline of you showing up every day to work something out *in* you, not just *for* you.

That's probably not the answer you wanted. But the point isn't performance. It's not, "If I do *this*, then God will do *that*."

Coming to the well every day demonstrates you know where your source is.

You're not trying to pull from your own strength. You're not trying to manufacture your own relief through willpower. You're acknowledging, "God, I need You today again, still."

Some seasons, the well doesn't remove your struggle. It simply sustains you through it.

You keep coming because that's where life is. Not because it guarantees you'll feel better immediately, but because it's where God meets you, nourishes you, and shows you He's with you even when you still feel forgotten.

Israel was in exile, spiritually parched, desperate for relief. They'd been drinking from that broken straw for a while.

And God said, "Come to the waters. Let Me show you what I can do when you stop trying to do it alone."

The choice point is right in front of you.
What will you choose?

***

IN THIS MOMENT

1. **Draw your own Choice Point.** On a piece of paper, draw a circle in the center. This is you at the choice point. Now draw two arrows coming out of the circle, one pointing up and to the right (label it "Toward God"), and one pointing down and to the left (label it "Away from God"). Where are you standing right now? What are you holding onto that's keeping you from moving toward Him?

2. **Identify what you're trying to hydrate with.** What are you reaching for instead of God? Success? Approval? Control? Distraction? Comfort? Name it specifically.

3. **Practice laying it down.** Write down one thing you've been carrying that you need to leave at the foot of the cross. Pray: "God, I can't carry this anymore. I'm giving it to You. Help me not pick it back up." Picture yourself laying that at the feet of Jesus. Then physically throw away the paper or tear it up as an act of release.

4. **Commit to drinking from the well tomorrow morning.** Before you check your phone, before you start your to-do list, open your Bible. Read one Psalm. Pray for 5 minutes.

Let God nourish you before the day demands everything from you.

***

OTHER MOMENTS

Is anyone thirsty? Come and drink—even if you have no money! Come, take your choice of wine or milk—it's all free! Why spend your money on food that does not give you strength? Why pay for food that does you no good? Listen to me, and you will eat what is good. You will enjoy the finest food. Come to me with your ears wide open. Listen, and you will find life. I will make an everlasting covenant with you. I will give you all the unfailing love I promised to David.

Isaiah 55:1-3

On the last day, the climax of the festival, Jesus stood and shouted to the crowds, "Anyone who is thirsty may come to me! Anyone who believes in me may come and drink! For the Scriptures declare, 'Rivers of living water will flow from his heart.'"

John 7:37-38

The Spirit and the bride say, "Come." Let anyone who hears this say, "Come." Let anyone who is thirsty come. Let anyone who desires drink freely from the water of life.

> Revelation 22:17

As the deer longs for streams of water, so I long for you, O God. I thirst for God, the living God. When can I go and stand before him?

> Psalm 42:1-2

Jesus replied, "Anyone who drinks this water will soon become thirsty again. But those who drink the water I give will never be thirsty again. It becomes a fresh, bubbling spring within them, giving them eternal life."

> John 4:13-14

DAY 10: The Whole Point Was Walking Together

"I will walk among you; I will be your God, and you will be my people."

— *Leviticus 26:12*

The book of Leviticus is quite a read. I'll confess it's a bit of a slow one for me. On the surface, it appears to be a book of do's and don'ts.

It unpacks God's covenant with Israel in some finer details, covering just about every part of daily life.

But much like the Bible itself, Leviticus is not just a collection of rules. It's the story of God providing a way for His creation to be with Him.

For Him to move and live among them.

The Problem of Holiness

Leviticus was written to a people who just escaped 400 years of slavery in Egypt.

They've seen God do some wild things: part the Red Sea, provide manna from heaven, and give them the Ten Commandments on Mount Sinai.

But they have no idea how to live as God's people. They don't know how to worship Him, approach Him, or maintain a relationship with Him.

So God gives them Leviticus, a detailed instruction manual for how to live in His presence.

But there's some tension here. God is perfectly holy. Sin cannot exist in His presence. Light and dark can't occupy the same space. His holiness is that pure. And sin is that destructive.

This isn't God being picky or mean. This is the reality of who He is.

Think of it like bringing a bucket of sewage into an operating room. It doesn't matter how much you need surgery, contamination and sterility can't coexist.

What All the Rules Were Really About

So Leviticus lays out an intricate system of sacrifices, offerings, and rituals.

There are rules about what to eat, how to dress, when to work, how to handle disease, how to conduct relationships, and how to approach God in worship.

And at the center of it all is the sacrificial system.

Sin offerings. Guilt offerings. Burnt offerings. Peace offerings. So many offerings. Each one serves a specific purpose in dealing with the barrier sin created.

Blood had to be shed and animals had to die. Priests had to mediate because they were set apart and purified to stand between God and the people.

It was costly and required constant absolute obedience to detailed instructions. But even with those countless lists of do's and don'ts, none of it was arbitrary.

Leviticus reads like a legal document because it IS one. But it's a love story written in legal language.

It's a detailed contract outlining how two parties can be together when everything should keep them apart. Every single rule, sacrifice, and ritual was a bridge across an impossible gap.

The Israelites couldn't just stroll into God's presence whenever they wanted. Sin had made that impossible.

But God wanted them close. More importantly, He wanted to walk among them. So He gave them a way. A costly, complicated way that required blood, constant attention, and obedience.

All those sacrifices pointed to something and someone bigger.

They weren't the ultimate solution. They served as a signpost pointing to Jesus. When Jesus came, He became the final sacrifice and the perfect Lamb. He was the ultimate High Priest.

He removed the stain of sin permanently without requiring all those endless rituals. You can only imagine how freeing that must've been for those who experienced life before Jesus and after.

It probably seemed too good to be true.

But that's grace. We didn't deserve it, but He wanted us.

The Greatest Love Story Ever Told

Every page of Leviticus, every offering, every priestly duty is to provide a way for us to be together with Him. His creation and the bearer of His own image.

His desire is for Him to be our God and for us to be His people.

That's the whole thing.

Leviticus is just another chapter in the greatest love story ever told. God could have left us in our sin. He could have written us off as a failed experiment.

But He didn't. Instead, He made a way.

From Garden to Tabernacle to Temple to... You

Remember the garden? God walked with Adam and Eve in the cool of the day. That was the original design. But sin destroyed that.

So God set up the tabernacle, then the temple. These were places where His presence could dwell among His people.

Granted, they were still separated by curtains and rituals and priests, but God's presence was there.

And then Jesus came. That changed the possibilities, because God doesn't just want to walk among His people anymore.

He wants to walk with you.

He Never Stopped Wanting You

God went to extraordinary lengths to make relationship possible. He could have simplified it or lowered the standard.

But He didn't, because sin is that serious and holiness is that pure. Instead, He made a way that honored both His holiness and His desperate desire to be with us.

Every rule in Leviticus says, "I want you close." Every sacrifice says, "I'm making a way." Every ritual says, "Don't give up. We can do this together."

And every single one of them pointed forward to Jesus, who would finally make it all permanent just so you could know Him.

Walking Together Now

You don't have to bring a lamb to the altar or wait for a priest to intercede. You don't have to wonder if you did the ritual correctly.

Jesus did it all. God can walk with you every single day, with no limitations, no matter where you are or what you've done.

The whole point, from Leviticus to the cross, was always about being together.

***

IN THIS MOMENT

1. **Read Leviticus 26:3-13.** As you read, underline, circle, or make a note of every time the passage describes God's proximity or presence. Notice how it builds from obedience to blessing to the climax: "I will walk among you."

2. **Picture God walking with Adam and Eve in the garden, just being with them.** That's what He wanted then. That's what He wants with you now. Write down what it would look like for you to walk in God's presence like that. What would you look at? What would you ask Him?

3. **The Israelites had to bring lambs, follow rituals, and go through priests to approach God.** Because of Jesus, you can talk to God whenever you want. Take a 2-minute walk right now and talk to Him like He's walking right next to you. Live out #2 in your life today.

4. **Practice His presence today.** Set three alarms on your phone. When they go off, pause and say out loud: "God, You're walking with me right now." Notice anything that changes for you.

***

OTHER MOMENTS

> I will live among you, and I will not despise you. I will walk among you; I will be your God, and you will be my people.
>
> Leviticus 26:11-12

> I will make my home among them. I will be their God, and they will be my people.
>
> Ezekiel 37:27

> So the Word became human and made his home among us. He was full of unfailing love and faithfulness. And we have seen his glory, the glory of the Father's one and only Son.
>
> John 1:14

> ...For we are the temple of the living God. As God said: "I will live in them and walk among them. I will be their God, and they will be my people."
>
> 2 Corinthians 6:16

And so, dear brothers and sisters, we can boldly enter heaven's Most Holy Place because of the blood of Jesus. By his death, Jesus opened a new and life-giving way through the curtain into the Most Holy Place. And since we have a great High Priest who rules over God's house, let us go right into the presence of God with sincere hearts fully trusting him. For our guilty consciences have been sprinkled with Christ's blood to make us clean, and our bodies have been washed with pure water.

Hebrews 10:19-22

I heard a loud shout from the throne, saying, "Look, God's home is now among his people! He will live with them, and they will be his people. God himself will be with them."

Revelation 21:3

DAY 11: You Can't Do This Alone

"And let us not neglect our meeting together, as some people do, but encourage one another, especially now that the day of his return is drawing near."

— Hebrews 10:25

You've spent 10 days building a habit of meeting with God.

You're reading Scripture and praying. You're practicing noticing His presence throughout your day.

And if you're honest, something may be starting to shift. You're noticing things you didn't before and feeling drawn to Him in ways you didn't think you could be.

But there's also this nagging feeling. Is this all there is? Just me and my Bible every morning? Shouldn't that be enough?

You're Not Meant to Do This Alone

Jesus is enough, yes, but God also designed you for relationship with others. You can't grow deep roots in isolation in your favorite reading chair at home.

You need community. You need people who will wrestle with Scripture alongside you, challenge you, ask you some hard questions at times, and run alongside you when life gets complicated. And some days, maybe bring you your favorite takeout meal.

The Christian life was never designed to be a solo journey.

In Romans 12:4-5, Paul writes: *"Just as our bodies have many parts and each part has a special function, so it is with Christ's body. We are many parts of one body, and we all belong to each other."*

You're one part of a body, not the whole body. Your left arm has a specific function but try to walk down a sidewalk using only your left arm. It won't work. You need your legs and hips to get where you want to go.

In the same way, in your isolation, you can't see your own blind spots or challenge your own assumptions. And you can't encourage yourself the way someone else can when you're ready to quit.

One of my favorite leadership roles was in a church where my husband and I led the new membership class. It was a four-week experience that connected new members with more established members of the church.

The group of about 30 people were assigned to specific leaders who sat at round tables together and got to know each person over that month.

They facilitated conversations about kids and grandkids, prayed with them after sharing some of their unique challenges, and ate a nice breakfast together on the fourth and final Sunday of the class.

From there, these new members had a springboard to launch into serving in a ministry in the church that used their specific gifts.

I can't tell you how many people told me before that first week that they weren't so sure about this class. That they really weren't "small group people" and preferred the anonymity of just the larger Sunday service.

Those same people walked away from that experience a month later at least knowing some names, and feeling more connected than just sitting on the pew or comfortable chair for an hour once a week.

Occasionally I run across a photo or two in my phone memories of young couples who became friends with others in the same season of life, or two people who became friendly enough that they attended the same Bible study together.

From this small group connection, they began the process of discipleship.

Where Real Growth Happens

The Sunday service isn't where discipleship happens. I'm not trying to throw shade to your senior pastor and his sermons, but hear me out.

Sunday services are designed for what's called *corporate worship*, where believers gather in a large group to be encouraged, and then be sent back out into the world.

This weekly gathering is important. God will use that hour or so to remind you of some things you may have forgotten since last Sunday, or confirm something you've already been thinking about.

And Sundays give you an opportunity to worship through music. God will speak to you through lyrics and when you sing of His glory through melodies that resonate with your spirit.

But real learning and transformation happens in these smaller settings because they allow you to be seen. They hold you accountable to contribute to the learning and encouragement of others in their journey.

This is where you can ask the questions you're afraid to ask in a big room. Where you can admit you don't understand something, or where someone further along can help you see what you're missing.

The Early Church Knew This

Acts 2:42 says the early believers *"devoted themselves to the apostles' teaching and to fellowship, and to sharing in meals (including the Lord's Supper), and to prayer."*

Notice the order: teaching, then fellowship.

They didn't just show up once a week to hear a sermon and leave. They met in homes and shared meals. They studied the Word together, they took communion together. Most importantly, they prayed for each other.

They weren't doing this because it was nice or because they enjoyed potlucks. They were doing it because they needed each other to survive.

The early church was persecuted in ways that are unfathomable to us now. The world's rulers wanted them dead. They had to figure out what it meant to follow Jesus in a world like that.

Without community, they wouldn't have made it.

You Won't Make It Either

You may not be running from Roman rulers like they were, but isolation is the enemy of transformation just the same.

We try hard to change on our own. We read books, listen to podcasts, and make detailed plans we try to hold ourselves to. But without some outside accountability, without people who know your patterns and can lovingly call you out, you drift back to old habits.

When I first meet with a new client, I assess for evidence of a support network. One question I ask is, "When you have a bad day, who is your first phone call?"

I can't tell you how many people tell me there is no one in their life they can unload the craziness of the day with. That's one of the first homework assignments I give them. Let's get you some connections.

You need people who will ask, "What has God shown you this week?" and actually wait for a real answer.

You need people who will notice when you don't show up for Bible study and call you to find out what's going on.

You need people who are a few steps ahead of you to show you what's possible.

And you need people right beside you to remind you you're not the only one struggling.

What to Look For

Don't make this a complicated search for the Holy Grail. Start with the church you're already attending. If you're not attending one, ask a Christian friend where they go. Chances are, they may have already invited you, so that's a great place to start.

Most churches have small groups or Bible studies that meet during the week. Look for a group that speaks to a particular interest or life stage, like a study of the book of Ruth, a men's group, or a group for young parents.

You'll find a mix of people, some who've been following Jesus for years, and some who are newer to the faith. You're not looking for Bible scholars who will go to the mat in biblical debates. Just find people committed to opening the Bible together and wrestling with what it says.

And here's the real key: show up consistently. Groups don't always gel in the first meeting or two. It takes several meetings to let your guard down and get to know people. Be patient with that process.

The Next Step

If you've read this far in the chapter, you've been building a habit for 11 days now. By the time you finish these 31 days, you'll have a solid rhythm of meeting with God in the morning.

But that's just the foundation.

Find a community where you can study the Bible with people who will challenge and encourage you, and discover the gifts God has given you by serving others.

Be an active member of the Body of Christ. You need others, and they need you just as much. God designed you so beautifully for relationship, first with Him, then with others who follow Him.

You've started the first part. Now it's time for the second. The walk with God that started in this quiet time needs to be lived out in community.

Now go find your people.

***

IN THIS MOMENT

1. **Today, find out if your church (or a church near you) has small groups or Bible studies.** Check their website, call the office, or ask someone on Sunday. Sign up for one that meets in the next two weeks.

2. **What are you afraid of when it comes to joining a group?** Being judged? Not knowing enough? Commitment? Write it down, then ask God to help you push past it.

3. **Think about your answer to the question:** "When you have a bad day, who is your first phone call?" If the answer is "no one," commit to changing that by joining a community where you can be known.

4. **Read Acts 2:42-47.** Notice how the early church did life together. What stands out to you? What would change if your faith looked more like that?

***

OTHER MOMENTS

So faith comes from hearing, that is, hearing the Good News about Christ.

Romans 10:17

All Scripture is inspired by God and is useful to teach us what is true and to make us realize what is wrong in our lives. It corrects us when we are wrong and teaches us to do what is right.

2 Timothy 3:16

Two people are better off than one, for they can help each other succeed. If one person falls, the other can reach out and help. But someone who falls alone is in real trouble.

Ecclesiastes 4:9-10

And all the believers met together in one place and shared everything they had.

Acts 2:44

DAY 12: The Rest is in God's Hands

"Then Jesus said, 'Come to me, all of you who are weary and carry heavy burdens, and I will give you rest.'"

— *Matthew 11:28*

We talk about rest like it's sleep. Or a vacation. Or a bubble bath.

Those things are good, you need them. But that's not the rest Jesus is talking about here.

The rest Jesus offers isn't about your body recovering from exhaustion.

It's about your spirit being relieved of striving.

What Is Striving?

I remember a particular phase in my life in big corporations where it felt like no matter what I did, I continued to stay behind. I always had a lot of work on my desk, and much of it was due yesterday when it was first assigned to me.

The idea of rest seemed preposterous because who could give up any time for that?

Most days, I stayed so late I needed a security guard to escort me to my car. Even when I was home, I chained myself to my laptop until my eyes bled. Neither seemed to move the needle at all.

I remember feeling so helpless and despairing. Clearly, I could work until I dropped, but it didn't seem to make any difference. There was always more to do.

The problem wasn't in my time management, or my ability to draw boundaries on how much work I could take on.

The problem is I was striving.

The Burden You Won't Give Up

Striving is trying to control outcomes you can't control. It's taking responsibility for things that aren't yours to fix.

Working yourself to the bone thinking that if you just try hard enough, it'll finally be enough.

But it never is. Because striving has no finish line. You will never complete the striving. Your own efforts won't relieve the burden and the pressure.

You can sleep eight hours and wake up still carrying the weight.

You can take a week off work and come back still anxious about everything that's not getting done.

You can practice all the self-care in the world and still feel like you're responsible for holding everything together.

Because the burden Jesus is talking about isn't physical fatigue. It's the weight of trying to be enough.

The Anxiety-Performance Loop

You feel anxious about not being enough, so you work harder to prove yourself. The harder you work, the more exhausted you become. The more exhausted you are, the less capable you feel. The less capable you feel, the more anxious you get about keeping up.

And so on, and so on.

Your nervous system stays in fight-or-flight mode worrying about it all. Your cortisol levels stay elevated like you're running from a grizzly bear, even though you're just sitting at your desk. Your body assumes you're under constant threat, so it never allows you to truly rest.

The clinical term is *burnout*. But what's really happening is you've convinced yourself that who you *are* depends on how well you *do* at everything.

That's hard enough for your mind to carry. Your body was never designed to carry that burden. It's a trap because you can never perform your way into being enough.

You won't feel rest until you can let that part go.

What God's Rest Actually Does

God's rest doesn't mean nothing hard happens or that you have no responsibilities.

It means you stop trying to carry them alone. You stop striving to be strong enough, smart enough, or capable enough on your own.

And you let Him carry it with you.

Rest Like God Rested

God rested on the seventh day after creating the heavens and the earth. But He didn't sleep. God doesn't need sleep. He doesn't get tired.

Genesis 2:2 says, *"On the seventh day God had finished his work of creation, so he rested from all his work."*

He released Himself from work. Look at that intention. Because He's God, He knew His efforts were enough. He didn't have anything to prove because the work was complete.

He wasn't exhausted, He was done. That's the rest He calls us to. Saying, "It's enough. I've done what I can do today. The rest is in God's hands."

Psalm 127:2 says, *"It is useless for you to work so hard from early morning until late at night, anxiously working for food to eat; for God gives rest to his loved ones."*

If you're a high performer the last thing you want to think is that your efforts are useless. Working like a fiend doesn't add a single thing. Striving doesn't make you more faithful. It just makes you exhausted.

Complete and Never Lacking

The rest Jesus gives is complete. It doesn't run out and it certainly doesn't depend on your circumstances improving. It's not contingent on you pulling levers in your own strength to get everything under control.

It's rest in the middle of the chaos. Peace that doesn't make sense given what you're facing. We're not promised that our circumstances will be any different.

But we can rest knowing that God is in the driver's seat.

Stop Striving, Start Resting

Stop carrying what He never asked you to carry. Stop striving to be enough on your own. Stop pushing through exhaustion thinking that the more tired you are the more faithful you are.

Matthew 6:27 says, *"Can all your worries add a single moment to your life?"*

Striving doesn't add anything. It just drains you. Let Him give you what you actually need to carry what's yours to carry.

That's the only true rest.

***

IN THIS MOMENT

1. **Make a list of everything you're carrying right now.**
   Work, family, responsibilities, worries, expectations. Write it

all down. Then go through the list and mark which burdens are yours to carry and which ones God never asked you to carry.

2. **Identify your anxiety-performance loop.** Where are you working harder because you feel anxious about not being enough? What outcome are you trying to control that isn't yours to control? Name it specifically.

3. **Practice releasing one burden to God right now.** Pick something on your list that you've been striving over. Say out loud, "This isn't mine to carry. I'm giving it to You." Practice again laying it at the foot of the cross. Thank Jesus for taking this burden for you.

4. **Notice where you're confusing exhaustion with faithfulness.** Are you wearing yourself out thinking that proves you're trying hard enough? Where do you need to stop striving and start resting? Choose an area to work on today.

***

OTHER MOMENTS

Take my yoke upon you. Let me teach you, because I am humble and gentle at heart, and you will find rest for your souls. For my yoke is easy to bear, and the burden I give you is light.

Matthew 11:29-30

The Lord is my shepherd; I have all that I need. He lets me rest in green meadows; he leads me beside peaceful streams. He renews my strength. He guides me along right paths, bringing honor to his name.

Psalm 23:1-3

This is what the Sovereign Lord, the Holy One of Israel, says: "Only in returning to me and resting in me will you be saved. In quietness and confidence is your strength...."

Isaiah 30:15

DAY 13: God Speaks in Stillness

"Be still, and know that I am God! I will be honored by every nation. I will be honored throughout the world."

— Psalm 46:10

When was the last time you just sat in a chair and watched the world go by?

We're not good at being still. In fact, we're terrible at it. There's always something to do. Something to fill the silence. Something to scroll.

Do you feel that one, too?

Being still feels dangerous and unproductive. What if you fall behind, then what? So you keep moving and keep your mind occupied with anything other than silence.

Stillness, though, will force you to confront things you may be avoiding.

In my work with clients, a defining moment can come in a session when a powerful emotion shows up.

The client might show visible signs of feeling pain, hurt, anger, confusion, or disappointment. Often they go quiet while they try to process what's happening. Like really quiet, for maybe a couple of minutes.

It's tempting in that moment to reach out and comfort them, or break the silence by offering comforting words.

But that stillness is working in the deepest parts of their soul and spirit. It's causing them to sit with that emotion and acknowledge how they've suffered, or what opportunities they may have missed.

It's important for them to have this experience. So I sit with them in the silence and just let it hang until the moment feels right.

It's uncomfortable to do this. Everything in me wants to break that stillness. But my training reminds me that my needs could keep that client from their work.

So I do my own work and sit with it, too.

That's what stillness does. It creates space for something real to surface. Something you've been too busy — or too afraid — to face.

Rest and Stillness Aren't the Same Thing

Day 12 was about rest, the relief from striving that comes when you stop carrying burdens you were never meant to carry.

Stillness is different than rest. Stillness is when you physically stop moving, doing, and filling every moment with noise and action.

Rest can happen while you're active. You can experience God's rest in the middle of a busy day. But stillness requires you to stop everything.

And the thought of that is terrifying for most of us.

Psalm 46:10 doesn't say, "Be still when everything's calm."

It says, *"Be still and know that I am God!"* in the middle of nations in uproar, kingdoms falling, and the earth giving way.

Stillness is choosing to stop moving in the middle of chaos so you can know God. That's when He reminds you that He's God.

God Will Never Shout Over Your Life

I've learned in more than five decades of walking with God, He will never shout over your life. He won't compete with your noise. He won't force His way into your chaos.

He talks to you in the stillness. Because that's when He knows you're actually listening for Him.

1 Kings 19 tells the story of Elijah running for his life, hiding in a cave after killing all the prophets of Baal (a refuge, perhaps?), and asking God to help this all make sense that His prophet would be in this predicament.

You can only imagine the internal narrative and rumination happening in Elijah's mind right now. He's restless for God to do something and feeling sorry for himself.

In 1 Kings 19:10 he says, *"I have zealously served the Lord God Almighty. But the people of Israel have broken their covenant with you, torn down your altars, and killed every one of your prophets. I am the only one left, and now they are trying to kill me, too."*

God brings him an answer, but not the way Elijah expected.

A powerful wind passed by so powerful it tore the mountains apart. But God wasn't in the wind.

Then, an earthquake came. But God wasn't in the earthquake. And last, a fire. But again, God wasn't in the fire.

After the fire got Elijah's attention came a gentle whisper. A still, small voice that said, "What are you doing here, Elijah?"

Elijah repeats his quandary to God, that everyone's after his blood. But then God gives Elijah specific, actionable instructions to anoint a new king of Israel, and a new prophet to replace Elijah.

God's next big step wasn't in the dramatic display. It was in the stillness after everything else stopped, including Elijah's desperate narrative.

Just like my clients who go quiet in session, Elijah had to stop his internal rumination before he could hear God's actual direction.

The wind, earthquake, and fire surely got his attention. But the whisper gave him the clarity he was looking for.

When you stop the narrative you've been telling yourself, God gives you what you actually need to hear.

What Stillness Reveals

God uses stillness to give you clarity because it removes the variables of your own action. If you're not moving, you're forced to pay attention to what's happening around you and in you, to be present and mindful.

Just like my clients in that quiet moment, when they stop trying to fill the space, that's when real work happens.

And like Elijah, that's when you hear the specific direction He has for you.

Maybe the reason you haven't heard from God is because you haven't been still long enough to listen. He doesn't need to send you earth, wind, and fire to get your attention.

Maybe He's waiting for you to stop and be still.

What to Do When Stillness Surfaces Something Hard

Let's be honest, stillness doesn't always feel peaceful. What surfaces can be painful: regret, grief, anger, fear you've been avoiding.

That's okay. God isn't revealing it to shame you. He's revealing it so you can finally give it to Him.

The emotions that surface in stillness are the ones you've been too busy to process. And God wants to heal them so you can move forward into what He has for you.

So when something uncomfortable comes up, resist the urge to fill the space with noise again. Name it, acknowledge it, and give it to God. He'll know what to do with it.

***

IN THIS MOMENT

1. **Set a timer for five minutes.** Sit in a chair with your feet on the floor and your hands in your lap. Close your eyes or stare at one spot. Notice how your body resists. Notice what thoughts come up. Notice what emotions surface. Don't judge yourself for them or do anything with them. Just name them silently: "anxiety," "restlessness," "sadness," "grief." Sit with them like I sit with my clients. Notice what it feels like to do this.

2. **Ask yourself:** What am I afraid will happen if I stop? Write down the first three things that come to mind. Those fears reveal what you're really trusting instead of God. Now look at the list and ask yourself if these fears are true, or if they are lies you've been believing?

3. **Schedule one 5-minute pocket of stillness in your day today.** Put it on your calendar with an alarm. When the time comes, go somewhere you won't be interrupted. Sit in silence. Don't pray, don't read Scripture, don't think about your to-do list. Be still and let God speak if He wants to.

4. **Read 1 Kings 19:11-13.** Notice how Elijah repeats the same complaint twice (v. 10 and v. 14). He's stuck in his narrative. God doesn't argue with him. He just gives him the next step. What narrative are you stuck in that's keeping you from hearing God's direction?

***

OTHER MOMENTS

Let all that I am wait quietly before God, for my hope is in him.

Psalm 62:5

But the Lord is in his holy Temple. Let all the earth be silent before him.

Habakkuk 2:20

The Lord is good to those who depend on him, to those who search for him. So it is good to wait quietly for salvation from the Lord.

Lamentations 3:25-26

DAY 14: You're Not Going to Blow It

"I take joy in doing your will, my God, for your instructions are written on my heart."

— *Psalm 40:8*

God knows me better than I know myself. He knew writing would delight me, so He's been giving me opportunities to write for as long as I can remember.

I've never had one specific destination for my writing. I've just followed where the words led.

And I believe I've been in God's will the whole time.

The Tightrope We've Created

We treat God's will like a tightrope. We've come to look at it as one narrow path with one exact destination and only one right answer.

And if we step off that path, even for a second, we're terrified that we'll fall off into the abyss. Then we'll have surely blown it. We're "out of God's will," a lost and wandering soul.

Now we have to claw our way back to that one perfect path before we can be useful again. I got exhausted just writing that.

It is an exhausting way to live, and it's not how God's will actually works.

God's Will Isn't a Destination

We've become obsessed with finding "God's will for my life" like it's a single address we have to locate on our maps app.

We must find the right job in the right city, where we find the right person to marry. We tag all that with trying to find the passion that drives it all.

The fear of making the right decision plagues us at every fork in the road. What if there's only one correct answer and everything else is wrong?

But look at Jesus. He had a destination. He was headed ultimately to the cross, resurrection, and ascension. He knew the destination and all the reasons for it.

But on the way, He taught in synagogues, spent time with children, had dinner with tax collectors, attended weddings, and rested with friends. Before His ministry years, He worked as a carpenter.

None of that was "off path." It was all part of doing His Father's will because it was part of Him participating in human life.

The Myth of the "Wrong Path"

We panic thinking we might be on the wrong path.

But Romans 8:28 says, *"And we know that God causes everything to work together for the good of those who love God and are called according to his purpose for them."*

God isn't wringing His hands because you took Job A instead of Job B. He's working with you and through you in Job A.

Proverbs 16:9 says, *"We can make our plans, but the Lord determines our steps."*

You make plans. Great, God directs.

You move. Whoa, what just happened? Don't worry, God also guides.

It's not about finding one magic path. It's about walking with Him wherever you are in whatever place your decisions brought you.

You Already Have His Approval

We get caught in the trap of thinking being "in God's will" means we've earned His good graces. Like if we make the right choices, He'll approve of us. And if we mess up, we've lost His favor.

But that's not how grace works.

Ephesians 2:8-9 says, *"God saved you by his grace when you believed. And you can't take credit for this; it is a gift from God. Salvation is not a reward for the good things we have done, so none of us can boast about it."*

You don't earn His love and approval. You can't. It's already yours, before you made any choice, and before you did anything right or wrong.

You're not working to stay in God's good graces. You're already there because of Jesus.

What God's Will Actually Is

So if God's will isn't about finding one perfect path and earning His approval, what is it?

It's simpler than you think.

God's will is that you trust Him.

1 Thessalonians 5:16-18 says, *"Always be joyful. Never stop praying. Be thankful in all circumstances, for this is God's will for you who belong to Christ Jesus."*

That's it. Joy, prayer, and gratitude, in all circumstances, even and especially in the most challenging ones.

God's will is that you glorify Him.

1 Corinthians 10:31 says, *"So whether you eat or drink, or whatever you do, do it all for the glory of God."*

Your job, your relationships, and your daily tasks all serve to reflect God's glory to others. The integrity you have at work, how you care for others who are going through life beside you, and the attention you pay to the mundane things of life demonstrate who He is to others.

God's will is that you tell others about Him.

Matthew 28:19-20 says, *"Therefore, go and make disciples of all the nations, baptizing them in the name of the Father and the Son and the Holy Spirit. Teach these new disciples to obey all the commands I have given you..."*

Your purpose isn't wrapped up in a vocation or a career, or even a specific set of gifts. It's to point people to Jesus, to reflect His character, and to share the story of what He's done for you.

Stop Panicking, Start Walking

You don't have to figure out The Plan with a capital P. You just have to take the next step He shows you.

He's already proven you don't need to walk a tightrope to be in relationship with Him.

He's walking with you every step of the way, and He'll show you the next part of the journey.

***

IN THIS MOMENT

1. **Identify one decision you're panicking about.** Write it down. Now ask: Am I afraid of making the "wrong" choice, or am I afraid God will be disappointed in me? Name which fear is actually driving you.

2. **Apply the three parts of God's will to this decision:**

    a. **Trust:** What would it look like to trust God with this outcome instead of trying to control it?

   b. **Glorify:** How can you glorify God in this decision, no matter which option you choose?

   c. **Tell:** How could this decision become an opportunity to point someone to Jesus?

3. **Read 1 Thessalonians 5:16-18.** This is God's will for you: joy, prayer, gratitude in ALL circumstances. Can you be joyful, prayerful, and grateful in either Option A or Option B? If yes, then you're not going to blow it.

4. **Take the next step in front of you today.** Write down what that step is and commit to doing it. God is directing your path even when you can't see the whole road (Proverbs 3:5-6).

***

OTHER MOMENTS

Trust in the Lord with all your heart; do not depend on your own understanding. Seek his will in all you do, and he will show you which path to take.

Proverbs 3:5-6

The Lord directs the steps of the godly. He delights in every detail of their lives. Though they stumble, they will never fall, for the Lord holds them by the hand.

Psalm 37:23-24

So we have not stopped praying for you since we first heard about you. We ask God to give you complete knowledge of his will and to give you spiritual wisdom and understanding. Then the way you live will always honor and please the Lord, and your lives will produce every kind of good fruit. All the while, you will grow as you learn to know God better and better.

Colossians 1:9-10

No, O people, the Lord has told you what is good, and this is what he requires of you: to do what is right, to love mercy, and to walk humbly with your God.

Micah 6:8

DAY 15: When You Can't Feel Him

"I am praying to you because I know you will answer, O God. Bend down and listen as I pray."

— *Psalm 17:6*

This verse shows the closeness David had with God. He prayed without hesitation because David knew God would answer.

When you speak to someone who loves you, they answer. I don't gasp in amazement when my husband responds to me. We're in a relationship. I expect him to respond. I don't wonder, as my words escape my lips, if I'll get an answer.

When you're in a relationship, it's not surprising when you hear the other person's voice. David had this kind of relationship with God.

Bending Down to Listen

Look at that phrase: *"Bend down and listen."*

That's not a distant God sitting high on a throne, barely aware of your existence. That's someone leaning in, getting close. That's a picture of them positioning themselves to hear every word.

When one of my grandsons is having a rough time, I sit in a chair and put my face at their level. I lean into them so our eyes are on the same plane. I can see their pain full on, and they can see GiGi's comforting face.

I speak into their pain, and let them know they're going to be okay. And of course, if a boo-boo is the culprit, Dr. GiGi is there to kiss that boo-boo away. After an interaction like this, there's no doubt in their mind that GiGi's got their back.

They are close enough to see it on my face and in my eyes.

We've Got the Picture Wrong

We've come to have this image of a faraway God sitting on a throne high above us, looking down on us silently while we pray. A God who is remote and distant, observing, but not interacting.

But the reality David knew is that God is right there with us. When we turn to look at Him, we see the One who has promised never to leave us, and who always responds according to His perfect wisdom and love.

And the minute we look at Him, we know He has our back. That's the kind of comfort David took refuge in. And it's available for us, too.

The Problem of Feeling

To be fair, sometimes you don't feel God close. You pray and hear nothing. You look for Him and see only emptiness. You're struggling, and that's exactly when you need to know He's near. But all you feel is alone.

That feeling — or lack of feeling — can be devastating.

If God is close, why can't I feel Him? Why does it seem like He's a million miles away?

Mother Teresa's Dark Night

Even Mother Teresa experienced this. After her death, her private journals revealed something shocking: she spent nearly 50 years feeling spiritually empty.

She described experiencing what's called "the dark night of the soul." This is a profound sense of God's absence that began fairly early in her ministry and never really left. She wrote about feeling like she'd lost God, and lost the warmth and consolation of His presence.

And yet she continued to serve and minister to the dying in Calcutta. She didn't stop pouring herself out for the poorest of the poor. She went fifty years without feeling God's presence, and still she continued to trust Him.

Feelings Aren't Facts

Acceptance and Commitment Therapy teaches a fundamental truth: thoughts and feelings aren't facts. They're experiences passing through you.

Imagine you are the sky. Clouds may float by, storms may come in, wind and rain may settle in for a day. These weather patterns will eventually move on because that's what they do. But the sky remains the same. The sky doesn't become a rain cloud just because it's raining.

You are not your emotions, you are the person experiencing them. And emotions, like the weather, will pass.

It's easy to over-identify with your emotions, to become fused with them until you and the emotion feel like one thing. When someone says "I'm an angry person" or "I'm an anxious person," that's fusion. In reality, you're a human having an angry or anxious experience, as many do. Those feelings can come and go because of your humanity.

You might feel abandoned, but that doesn't mean you are abandoned.

You might feel unheard, but that doesn't mean God isn't listening.

Your feelings are real and they're valid. But they're not reliable reporters of reality.

Feelings are influenced by sleep deprivation, stress, hormones, past trauma, and a hundred other variables that have nothing to do with God's actual presence.

In ACT, we use *cognitive defusion to* create distance between yourself and your emotions. You observe them, allow them to exist, then let them go. This serves to keep those thoughts and feelings from having as much power over you, to control you.

Instead of "I feel abandoned by God, therefore I am abandoned," you learn to say: "I'm *having the feeling* of being abandoned by God."

It's a subtle shift, but it changes your perspective.

Mother Teresa felt God's absence for fifty years. But she didn't let that feeling dictate her theology or her actions.

She kept serving because she knew her feelings weren't telling her the truth about God's presence. She acted on what God had already shown her to be true about Him.

Her story is a powerful reminder that you don't have to feel God to still be used by Him. You don't have to feel Him to impact other people. And you don't have to feel Him to trust that He's actually there.

Deuteronomy 31:8 says, *"Do not be afraid or discouraged, for the Lord will personally go ahead of you. He will be with you; he will neither fail you nor abandon you."*

None of that is contingent on whether or not you feel his presence in a warm, tangible way. He promises to be there whether you get goosebumps or not.

Even When You Don't Feel Him

So if you're in a season where you can't feel God, know this: You're not alone. You're not abandoned. You're not forgotten.

Mother Teresa still changed the world because she trusted what she knew was true over what she felt.

David knew God was close not because he always felt warm fuzzies, but because God had proven Himself faithful again and again.

You may not feel Him right now. But He's bending down and leaning in.

He's close enough to hear every word.

And He's got your back.

***

IN THIS MOMENT

1. **Write down one time when God proved faithful to you.** A time when you saw His hand clearly, when you knew He was there. Hold onto that memory when feelings fail, that's evidence, not emotion.

2. **Practice cognitive defusion right now.** Identify one negative feeling you're having about God's presence (or lack of it). Instead of "God has abandoned me," reframe it: "I'm *having the feeling that* God has abandoned me." Say it out loud. Notice how the feeling loses some of its power when you create distance from it.

3. **Use the sky metaphor this week.** When a difficult emotion comes up, picture yourself as a blue sky and that feeling as weather passing through. Watch the weather move out of your mind's eye.

4. **Read Psalm 139:7-10**. Meditate on the fact that there's nowhere you can go where He isn't, even when you can't feel it. This is theological truth that stands whether you feel it or not.

***

OTHER MOMENTS

> The Lord is close to the brokenhearted; he rescues those whose spirits are crushed.
> Psalm 34:18

> Come close to God, and God will come close to you...
> James 4:8

> The Lord is close to all who call on him, yes, to all who call on him in truth.
> Psalm 145:18

> Don't love money; be satisfied with what you have. For God has said, "I will never fail you. I will never abandon you."
> Hebrews 13:5

DAY 16: Who Gets Your First Words?

"Let me hear of your unfailing love each morning, for I am trusting you. Show me where to walk, for I give myself to you."

— Psalm 143:8

You woke up this morning and the first thing you probably did was reach for your phone. Before you even opened your eyes all the way or spoke to anyone in your house, you scrolled.

Instagram. TikTok. The news. Email. Whatever algorithm has learned to grab your attention first.

You got pulled into a swarm of posts and memes that feed your need for validation. Your brain learns the pattern and craves more the minute you put the phone down.

And just like that, the first moments of your day belonged to everyone else.

The Dopamine Trap

Social media apps are designed to trigger dopamine release. This is the same neurotransmitter involved in addiction. Every notification, like, comment, or new post gives you a little hit.

Your brain learns phone = reward. Over time, you develop a craving. The moment you wake up, your brain says, "Check your phone. You don't want to miss something."

But finding out what you missed doesn't satisfy you. It just creates the need to seek more. Think about it, do you ever feel content after scrolling? No, you just feel compelled to keep scrolling.

That's why you can spend 30 minutes on your phone and still feel restless, anxious, or empty.

It's tempting to think you're weak or undisciplined. To be fair, you're up against billion-dollar companies that have engineered their apps to produce as much of this dopamine as possible.

And they're winning the battle for your first attention every single day. What must this look like from God's perspective?

Good morning, God!

Picture a young toddler dressed in the cutest Baby Shark pajamas, sweetly waking up in their crib.

Standing in the hall near their door, you hear their adorable sounds. Maybe they're singing the Baby Shark song with half the words missing.

You smile and shake your head, you're so excited to start the day together.

You hear your toddler giggling between refrains of Mommy and Daddy Shark. After a while, you can't stand it anymore, and you open the door, arms wide, ready to scoop them up for a "Good morning!"

But when you burst in the room, they don't even look at you.

Turns out, they were watching Baby Shark on a phone and singing along wide-eyed at the screen. They were completely absorbed in what musical strangers have put in front of them before you got in there.

You say "Good morning!" again. They give you kind of a side glance and a wisp of a smile, but their face is quickly drawn back down. They know you're there, but they're torn. They're so engrossed in the music and images that they have trouble keeping their attention on you.

They love you, but they just don't realize what they're missing by not looking up.

The first hug. The connection with you when your attention is freshest. The excitement of telling them what amazing thing you were going to do today.

That's What We Miss

God isn't angry that you picked up your phone first this morning. He just knows what He wanted to give you in those first moments. And

He knows you traded His presence, with its grace and mercy for today, for anxiety about things you have no role in and can't control.

Lamentations 3:22-23 (NIV) says, *"Because of the Lord's great love we are not consumed, for his compassions never fail. They are new every morning; great is your faithfulness."*

He shows up fresh for you every single day with exactly what you need for that day. But if you fill your mind with everyone else's words first, it's harder to hear His.

Social media in particular is engineered to appeal to something in us that feels urgent. Most of what we consume first thing in the morning has nothing to do with what God has for us that day. It's related to what we've tried to create for ourselves to feel validated.

What God Wants to Give You

God knows what you're facing today before you even know it. He knows the conversation that's going to be hard for you to navigate. The decision you'll have to make that won't please anyone. The moment you'll need His peace to get through the afternoon.

Dopamine gives you a hit, then leaves you empty. God gives you peace, wisdom, and direction.

The phone promises connection but delivers anxiety. God promises presence and actually shows up with exactly what you need for this day.

Psalm 5:3 says, *"Listen to my voice in the morning, Lord. Each morning I bring my requests to you and wait expectantly."*

The morning is when you set the trajectory for your day. It's the perfect time to let God orient you before the world starts demanding things from you.

So How Do You Actually Do This?

We think we need a specific duration and a vibe for it. Keep it simple. Start with ten minutes. Open your Bible and read one Psalm or one chapter of Proverbs.

Then ask God: "What do You want me to know today?"

Be Still, and Listen

You don't even have to get out of bed to do this. But you give Him first access when you do. When I give God those first ten minutes, scrolling after feels like background noise.

God might speak through a scripture quote that scrolls past or a post from someone who says exactly what you need to hear. But these encounters work best as echoes of what you've already heard from Him directly, not in place of it.

The first voice you hear in the day will be the confirming voice you hear for the rest of your day.

Every Morning is a Choice.

Who gets your first attention? The God who gave you this day and knows exactly what you need?

Or the algorithm engineered to make you feel "less than" and hungry scrolling for validation?

You might be surprised by what you've been missing.

***

IN THIS MOMENT

1. **Tonight, do this before bed:** Put your phone in another room, in a drawer, or across the bedroom, anywhere you can't reach it from bed. Put your Bible on your nightstand instead. If you use your phone as an alarm, buy a $10 alarm clock. This one change removes a big part of the battle in the morning.

2. **Tomorrow morning, before you touch your phone, say this out loud:** "Good morning, God. I'm here. What do You have for me today?" Say it even if you don't feel it, maybe especially if you don't feel it.

3. **Set a timer for 10 minutes.** Open your Bible to Psalm 143 or Psalm 5. Read it out loud. If someone's in the room with you, read it to them. After you read, ask God: "What do You want me to know today?" Write down anything that comes to mind.

4. **After your 10 minutes with God, notice how you feel when you do pick up your phone.** Does the scroll feel different? Does the news hit differently? Are you reaching for it with the same urgency? Is it a little easier to put it down when it's time to move on? Write down what you notice.

5. **Try this for one week.** At the end of seven days, count how many mornings you chose God first. What made the difference on the days you succeeded? What derailed you on the days you didn't? What would it take to make this your

new normal? Write down your reflections on those answers.

***

OTHER MOMENTS

The faithful love of the Lord never ends! His mercies never cease. Great is his faithfulness; his mercies begin afresh each morning.

Lamentations 3:22-23

Satisfy us in the morning with your unfailing love, that we may sing for joy to the end of our lives.

Psalm 90:14

Let me hear of your unfailing love each morning, for I am trusting you. Show me where to walk, for I give myself to you.

Psalm 143:8

DAY 17: When Worry Tries to Do God's Job

"That is why I tell you not to worry about everyday life—whether you have enough food and drink, or enough clothes to wear. Isn't life more than food, and your body more than clothing?"

— *Matthew 6:25*

My mom has this verse framed and hanging on a wall in her kitchen. She says it reminds her that she's so blessed she can just open the refrigerator or pantry and get whatever food she wants.

We're not to worry about the basic things in life. God has us covered for what we need when we need it. He promised it long ago.

Everything we need comes in His time and His providence. Our job is simply to trust.

But We Worry Anyway

We just can't help ourselves, it seems. Even though we know God promises to provide, we still worry.

About money or bills, or whether we'll have enough to cover what's coming. Or food, housing, healthcare, all the everyday necessities that pile up faster than we can keep track of.

Worry sets up camp in your head, and once it's there, it's hard to evict.

As a therapist, I see this all the time. People get caught in the spin cycle, worrying about how they'll handle everything before it even gets here.

It's not just the big crises. It's the everyday things, too. Will there be enough left over? Will it work out in the end? What if it doesn't?

The Control Underneath the Worry

A lot of that worry comes from wanting to control exactly how things get taken care of. We very much want things to go our way.

We want to see the plan and buy in to the timeline. We want a crystal ball for exactly how it's all going to work out. And when we can't see it, we panic.

Because if we can't control it, how can we be sure it'll happen? But that question reveals what — or who — we're really trusting.

What Worry Actually Does to You

Many of my clients get caught in what's called *catastrophic thinking*. I call this the end-of-the-world syndrome, where you imagine the worst-case scenarios and treat them as inevitable.

Your brain doesn't distinguish between real threats and imagined ones. When you worry about something that might happen, your body responds as if it's happening right now.

Cortisol floods your system to get you ready to flee. Your heart rate increases, your muscles tense. Your body's in full go-mode over a bill that isn't even due yet.

This is what Jesus meant when He asked, *"Can all your worries add a single moment to your life?"*

The answer is no. Worry doesn't prepare you for the future. All it does is exhaust you in the present and take away your power to prepare for a more likely outcome.

And besides, most of what we worry about never happens. Studies show that 85% of what people worry about never comes to pass. You're draining your best cognitive energy over imaginary problems while God is trying to provide for actual needs.

God Provides in His Way

When I was newly married, my husband and I were living on very little. Our bills were $800 a month back then. That doesn't sound like much now, but when you're scraping by like we were, it might as well have been $8,000.

We were good at finding resources to pay those bills. We could work hard and put that budget together.

But sometimes when things were tight, we'd try to double down on our own resources. We'd cut more corners, or borrow from one area to pay another. It felt like we were always coming in hot to the end of the month with nothing left over.

All that would add up to some real stress, even when we were able to take care of things. Sometimes it just felt so hard putting it all together.

How Much Did We Miss?

Looking back on that time, I've wondered how many times we didn't let Him provide for us. How many times did we try to do it in our own strength and miss out on what He had planned?

It's not like God's provision didn't have some precedent in our lives. When we were first dating, we were so broke we couldn't come up with two quarters to buy something from the vending machine in the study hall in college.

One afternoon we ransacked the couches for loose change and peered under tables and desks for any runaway coins. No luck. We resigned ourselves to our hunger, then heard a loud "ka-ching, ka-ching" from the vending machine.

My then-fiance walked over to the machine and checked the coin return. He smiled and fished out two brand-new shiny quarters, gleaming like two treasure coins. It was exactly what we needed, when we needed it. We didn't even have time to worry about it.

We've talked about that afternoon so many times through the years. Before we even married, God was trying to tell us that He would take care of us. Why did we ever insist on trying to do it in our own power?

We were so busy white-knuckling our own solutions that we couldn't see His.

The Birds and the Flowers Know

Jesus knew we'd struggle with this. That's why He gave us such a clear picture.

Matthew 6:26-30 says, *"Look at the birds. They don't plant or harvest or store food in barns, for your heavenly Father feeds them. And aren't you far more valuable to him than they are? Can all your worries add a single moment to your life? And why worry about your clothing? Look at the lilies of the field and how they grow. They don't work or make their clothing, yet Solomon in all his glory was not dressed as beautifully as they are. And if God cares so wonderfully for wildflowers that are here today and thrown into the fire tomorrow, he will certainly care for you. Why do you have so little faith?"*

If God takes care of birds and flowers, how much more will He take care of you? You don't ever see birds freaking out about tomorrow's meals. Flowers don't stress about having what they need to look good.

They just eat and grow because God does all the heavy lifting for them.

Worry Doesn't Add a Single Moment

Jesus asks the question directly: *"Can all your worries add a single moment to your life?"*

Worry doesn't create provision. It doesn't solve problems, and it doesn't add anything. It just flat out steals your peace.

Worry is effort without result. You're working so hard mentally and emotionally, spinning your wheels, exhausting yourself trying to cover all your bases. And none of it changes the outcome.

God is going to provide either way. The question is whether you'll trust Him and experience peace, or worry and miss the peace He's offering.

Do What You Can, Let God Do the Rest

Stop trying to control what you can't control. Stop worrying about variables that aren't yours to manage.

Do what you can, then let God do the rest. That's where you'll find His provision waiting.

My mom gets it. That verse on her kitchen wall reminds her to do what she can and trust God for the rest. She opens the refrigerator grateful, not anxious, because she knows who's really providing.

He has a track record. And He thinks of your needs before you do.

***

IN THIS MOMENT

1. **Make a list of everything you're worrying about providing right now.** Bills, needs, resources, upcoming expenses, financial decisions. Write them all down. Don't hold back, get every worry on paper, even the ones that feel too small to mention.

2. **Go through the list and mark each item with either "I

can act" or "Out of my control." For every "I can act" item, write down one specific action you can take today. Now do that action. Make the call, send the email, pay the bill, whatever it is. Then physically cross off everything marked "Out of my control" and say out loud: "This is God's to handle, not mine."

3. **Look out the window at birds today for at least 5 minutes.** Notice how they go about getting their food. If you're close enough, look at their faces. Do they look worried? If it's winter, how do they move differently knowing fewer resources are available? Write down what you observe about them. What do they seem to be doing instead of worrying?

4. **Write down one specific time God provided for you unexpectedly.** Use these prompts: What did you need? How desperate did it feel? How did God provide? What was your reaction when it happened? Keep this story somewhere visible where you can fish it out like those two quarters from the vending machine. When worry creeps in this week, reread it. Let it remind you: He's done it before. He'll do it again.

5. **At the end of this week, look at your "Out of my control" list again.** How many of those things did God handle? How many resolved themselves? How many are you still carrying that you need to release again? Write down what you learned about worry vs. trust.

***

OTHER MOMENTS

And this same God who takes care of me will supply all your needs from his glorious riches, which have been given to us in Christ Jesus.

Philippians 4:19

Once I was young, and now I am old. Yet I have never seen the godly abandoned or their children begging for bread.

Psalm 37:25

And don't be concerned about what to eat and what to drink. Don't worry about such things. These things dominate the thoughts of unbelievers all over the world, but your Father already knows your needs. Seek the Kingdom of God above all else, and he will give you everything you need.

Luke 12:29-31

DAY 18: When Everything That's Broken Gets Fixed

"But we are looking forward to the new heavens and new earth he has promised, a world filled with God's righteousness."

— *2 Peter 3:13*

P art of my experience growing up in church was singing hymns.

Hymns were songs written by sometimes very prolific composers and lyricists that told a story of what God meant to them, or celebrated how He had brought them through something.

One such hymn was called "When We All Get to Heaven." It was written by Eliza Hewitt, as a collaboration with composer Emily Wilson. I remember it for its exuberant melody but the words were also vivid.

When we all get to heaven, What a day of rejoicing that will be! When we all see Jesus, We'll sing and shout the victory!

Eliza was a teacher, and had been injured by a student who struck her with a heavy slate. The spinal damage she suffered left her bedridden and in pain for years.

Hewitt wrote this song as a personal meditation of heaven, where she would one day no longer suffer pain.

Songs like these spoke of what those in Christ were destined for. Christians who sang these hymns understood this life was so very temporary.

They were a constant reminder of our most important priorities while we're here because we tend to chase things that won't survive eternity.

Hymns painted a picture that Christians could look forward to when they struggled. One day, all our needs are met. Everything that's wrong is right. We're restored to a perfect relationship with the One who created us.

The desperate search ends. That empty space in our heart is finally filled with Him for eternity.

It seems like we've turned that vision upside down.

We're Focused on the Wrong Thing

Somewhere along the way, we've turned life with Christ into more of a self-help program than a journey that ends in the ride of our lives.

Come to Jesus and your marriage will improve. Your finances will stabilize. Your anxiety will disappear. Follow these steps, apply these principles, and watch your life transform.

And yes, walking with Jesus does change your life now. But if that's all we're offering, we've reduced the gospel to a life-coaching program with better branding.

The Christian life isn't primarily about making your life on earth better. It's about getting you ready for an eternity with God and bringing as many with you as possible.

Why We Struggle with Eternal Perspective

Anxiety is worrying about the future. But the problem is that we're anxious about the wrong future.

You worry about next month's bills, your health in five years, your financial security for your senior years. Your mind is constantly spinning scenarios about what might go wrong in one of those timeframes.

This is called *future-oriented anxiety*, where your brain is stuck in tomorrow's problems instead of today's reality.

Ironically, focusing on eternity is a great cure for temporal anxiety. When you truly grasp that this life is a blip and eternity is what's real, it recalibrates what actually matters.

You realize that in light of the vastness of eternity, the bills, the diagnoses, and the conflicts are all temporary. Having an eternal perspective puts them in proper scale.

You can address what needs attention today without being destroyed by anxiety about tomorrow because you know where this is all headed.

That's why hymns like Eliza Hewitt's were so popular. They pulled people out of temporal anxiety and reminded them that suffering is real but it's not the ultimate state of mind. Keep your eyes on what's coming.

This World is Not Your Home

Everything you're dealing with right now isn't where this ends. Our life is a vapor that dissipates in a brief moment.

James 4:14 says, *"How do you know what your life will be like tomorrow? Your life is like the morning fog—it's here a little while, then it's gone."*

Your entire life on earth, even if you live to be 100, is a blip compared to eternity.

I saw a sermon recently where the pastor brought a 100-foot-long rope onto the stage.

The first foot or so of that rope was wrapped in bright red tape. The rest of it stretched across the stage and lay coiled high at the other end. He held up the red portion as an illustration of our life on earth.

Everything happens in that tiny space: first kiss, wedding day, the birth of your children, career highs and lows, retirement, and then, death.

All of it contained in that red-wrapped foot of rope, while eternity stretches hundreds of feet beyond.

An eternity with a new heaven and a new earth, where we get new bodies that don't decline or decay, and perfect relationship with God.

That's what's coming. But what will it actually be like?

God's Full Presence on Display

If the same God who spoke galaxies into existence is recreating heaven and earth, we can't even begin to imagine what that will look like.

How much more amazing will our perfect, glorified bodies be without pain, sickness, or decay? We will stand in the full presence of God. The glory that our bodies can't sustain now will be what sustains us then.

Revelation 21:23 says, *"And the city has no need of sun or moon, for the glory of God illuminates the city, and the Lamb is its light."*

We'll no longer look to the sun's rising and setting to orient our days. The glory of God will be all the light we need.

I think that will be pretty wild.

What We've Forgotten

Eliza Hewitt understood this. So did Christians throughout history who suffered unimaginable persecution, martyrdom, poverty, and loss.

They were able to endure because they kept their eyes firmly on eternity. They weren't chasing comfort now, but they were holding on to the promise of forever.

When we all get to heaven, what a day of rejoicing that will be.

Eliza Hewitt was right. When the days seem hopeless, don't lose sight of what's coming.

No more tears. No more death. No more pain.

Just Him and you, and all your needs finally, fully, completely, eternally met.

That's what we're looking forward to.

***

IN THIS MOMENT

1. **Read Revelation 21:1-7 and 2 Peter 3:13.** Write down one phrase that stands out to you. No more death, no more tears, God dwelling with His people. Now ask: What pain in my life right now would be healed by this promise?

2. **Write down one specific pain or struggle you're dealing with right now.** Then complete this sentence: "In eternity, this will be healed because _____." Be specific about what changes.

3. **Draw a horizontal timeline of your life.** Mark major events with hashmarks (birth, graduation, marriage, kids, whatever matters to you). Put an X where you are right now. Then extend the line into eternity. Make it at least 3x longer than your earthly timeline and label it "Forever with God." Look at the proportion. What does this do to how you view your current struggles?

***

OTHER MOMENTS

But we are citizens of heaven, where the Lord Jesus Christ lives. And we are eagerly waiting for him to return as our Savior. He will take our weak mortal bodies and change them into glorious bodies like his own, using the same power with which he will bring everything under his control.

Philippians 3:20-21

It is the same way with the resurrection of the dead. Our earthly bodies are planted in the ground when we die, but they will be raised to live forever. Our bodies are buried in brokenness, but they will be raised in glory. They are buried in weakness, but they will be raised in strength. They are buried as natural human bodies, but they will be raised as spiritual bodies. For just as there are natural bodies, there are also spiritual bodies.

1 Corinthians 15:42-44

Since you have been raised to new life with Christ, set your sights on the realities of heaven, where Christ sits in the place of honor at God's right hand. Think about the things of heaven, not the things of earth.

Colossians 3:1-2

He will wipe every tear from their eyes, and there will be no more death or sorrow or crying or pain. All these things are gone forever.

Revelation 21:4

DAY 19: When "Good Enough" Costs You God's Best

"If we have found favor with you, please let us have this land as our property instead of giving us land across the Jordan River."

— *Numbers 32:5*

After 40 years in the wilderness, Israel is finally camped on the east side of the Jordan River. The Promised Land is right there. Just across the water.

Everything they've been waiting for and everything God promised Abraham, Isaac, and Jacob. This is what their parents died without seeing because of their unbelief.

But the land east of the Jordan — the land they've already conquered — is excellent for livestock.

Two and a half Israelite tribes look around and think, You know, this is pretty good, too. Why cross over when we could just settle here?

The Ask That Changes Everything

The tribes of Reuben and Gad, along with half of Manasseh, approach Moses with a request.

"Can we just stay here? This land is perfect for our herds. We'd rather settle on this side."

Moses is immediately worried and maybe a little triggered. This sounds like the rebellion that kept their parents out of Canaan for 40 years. After coming this far, are we really doing this? Is this going to discourage the whole nation again?

But they promise, "We'll send our fighting men across with everyone else. We'll help conquer the land first. Then we'll come back and settle here."

They must've been in good standing with Moses because he agrees, albeit with conditions. If they fail, they won't just be letting their nation down. They'll be sinning against God.

And God allows it.

God Often Grants What We Ask For

This seems off the beaten path, but God didn't say *no*. He gave them what they wanted. Good land, security for their wives and children, pastures for their livestock, everything they asked for.

It wasn't sin or rebellion. But it was... less.

Less than what God had imagined for them in the heart of the land He'd promised to them generations ago.

What They Missed

They got what they wanted right now, without waiting for what God had planned. And in the moment, it probably felt like a pretty good idea.

Why take a risk on the unknown when you can have something good that's already right here? But they did give up some things that would create issues for them over time.

- The central place of worship where God's presence would dwell.

- Deeper spiritual unity with the rest of Israel.

- Geographic protection from the more fortified group.

- The fuller inheritance God intended, right in the middle of everything He was doing.

They got good, but they missed God's best. Over time, they became more vulnerable, distant, and disconnected from what God was building. They chose immediate comfort over future promise.

And God let them.

We Set Our Own Limits

God is gracious enough to give us what we ask for, even when it's less than His best. He doesn't force us into His fuller blessing. He will defer to our free will and won't override our choice for "good enough."

Romans 8:28 says, *"And we know that God causes everything to work together for the good of those who love God and are called according to his purpose for them."*

God can work with whatever we choose. He's that good. But that doesn't mean every choice we make leads to the same outcome.

Where Do You Settle?

Think about your life right now. What have you settled for because it felt safer than trusting God for more?

- The job that pays the bills but doesn't really use the gifts God gave you.

- The relationship that's comfortable but not what you know God has called you to.

- The town you stayed in because moving felt like too much of a risk.

- The dream you let go of because the long path that leads to it seemed too overwhelming.

These choices aren't sinful necessarily. God won't condemn you for choosing safety over His best.

But settling will cost you the fuller story God wanted to write with your life.

Why We Settle

I see this pattern more consistently than any other with my clients, especially when it comes to relationships.

A client stays with someone who's emotionally unavailable, inconsistent, or not as invested as they are. When I gently ask why they're sticking around, the answer is almost always the same:

"What if I don't find something better?"

The fear of being alone feels more threatening than the reality of being unfulfilled. So they settle because "good enough" feels safer than risking the unknown.

This *loss aversion* means we're more motivated to avoid loss than to pursue gain. Sure, the relationship isn't great, but leaving means losing what you do have. The job isn't so fulfilling, or it's stagnant, but quitting means losing security. What then?

So you stay on the east side of the Jordan, building a life around what's "pretty good" instead of crossing the river toward what God says is yours.

This catches up with you after a few seasons when you realize every day you spend settling is a day you're not available for God's best.

"Good Enough" Is Still a Choice

Reuben, Gad, and half of Manasseh chose visible comfort over faith-required promise. They chose to build their lives on what they could see and control instead of what God had said for a generation was waiting across the river.

And God gave them exactly what they asked for. But years later, when the kingdom split and enemies came, those tribes were the first to fall. They were geographically and spiritually distant from the heart of what God was doing.

This was the cost of the easier path at the beginning.

God Won't Force You

God is too kind to force you into His best. He lets you choose. He'll work with whatever you give Him. But He knows what you're missing when you settle.

And He's inviting you to trust Him for more.

***

IN THIS MOMENT

1. **Ask yourself:** Where have I settled for "good enough" instead of trusting God for His best? Look for specific areas in your career, relationship, living situation, ministry opportunity, or creative calling. Journal the insights you get.

2. **Pick one of these areas and identify where you chose safety over faith:** What made that feel like the right choice at the time? What fear was driving that choice?

3. **What's your "land east of the Jordan?"** In which of these areas are you trying to negotiate to settle? What looks really good *right now* that might be keeping you from crossing into

what God has next? Complete this sentence: "This is good, but God's best for me is _____."

4. **Consider the cost:** Draw a line down the middle of a page. Label the left side, "If I stay here" and list what staying costs you long-term. Label the right side, "If I cross the Jordan" and list what it would cost you to pursue God's best (what would you risk? what would you have to trust God for?). Now look at both columns. Which cost is actually higher?

5. **Pray this:** "God, show me where I've settled. Show me where I've chosen comfort over Your best. Give me courage to trust You for more. Show me what's on the other side of the Jordan that I can't see from here." Write down anything that comes to mind as you pray.

***

OTHER MOMENTS

Trust in the Lord with all your heart; do not depend on your own understanding. Seek his will in all you do, and he will show you which path to take.

Proverbs 3:5-6

"For I know the plans I have for you," says the Lord. "They are plans for good and not for disaster, to give you a future and a hope."

Jeremiah 29:11

Now all glory to God, who is able, through his mighty power at work within us, to accomplish infinitely more than we might ask or think.

Ephesians 3:20

It was by faith that Abraham obeyed when God called him to leave home and go to another land that God would give him as his inheritance. He went without knowing where he was going.

Hebrews 11:8

DAY 20: The Difference Between "I Did Wrong" and "I Am Wrong"

"Fear not; you will no longer live in shame. Don't be afraid; there is no more disgrace for you. You will no longer remember the shame of your youth..."

— *Isaiah 54:4*

God stamped this Bible verse on my heart. No more shame, no more disgrace.

I've struggled with shame most of my life. You may have, too. There's almost no worse feeling than the one that tells you you're not enough.

Thinking you've made so many mistakes you could never be useful.

You see how easy it's been for others to take advantage of you, and you were the one who straight-up handed them the keys.

And the worst part is you see how many opportunities you were afraid to take on because you couldn't imagine living past your pain.

Fear loves to ride shotgun with shame. But God is not a God of fear. Or shame.

If I truly trust God, then I believe what He says is true. So if He says my shame days are over, I have to start living like it.

So why is it still so hard to shake this feeling that you've done something wrong?

Guilt And Shame Are Not The Same

Have you ever had an important conversation with someone to let them know how their actions affected you? Even if they agreed with you, no doubt they might've pushed back with all the things you did wrong, too.

Walking away from that experience, this guilty feeling sets in. Yet you can't quite put your finger on what you did wrong, but you feel wrong.

That might be shame setting in.

Guilt tells you when you've done something wrong.

Guilt establishes a clear consequence. If you've done something wrong, you'll need to pay some kind of restitution.

For example, if you drive 75 mph in a 55-mph-zone, and you get pulled over, guess what? You're guilty. Who you are as a person doesn't really matter. The reality is, you broke the law.

Most likely, you'll get a fine. You can own it, take care of it, tell your friends how unfair it was, and move on.

Guilt is about your actions and the consequences that may result.

Shame tells you that you ARE something wrong.

It will try to convince you the person you are, and are trying to be, is making everyone around you miserable. Shame will whisper in your ear that if only you were better, everyone else would be better.

Shame will dress itself up like guilt and try to convince you that you owe restitution for something you're not actually guilty of.

Shame goes after your identity.

When Shame Masquerades as Guilt

Go back to that important conversation with someone. What was going through your mind when you walked away from that interaction?

Who do you think you are to limit their access to speak into your life however they want? Do you really think you're so much better than them? Who gave you the right to talk to people like that?

That "who-do-you-think-you-are" voice isn't guilt, it's shame.

If you've truly injured someone, own your part, acknowledge it, and build a bridge to restore trust. But that icky feeling that comes after protecting yourself is not guilt asking you to make amends. That's shame telling you you're wrong for having needs.

Shame tries to lure you into a pointless game of "stop hitting yourself." Shut that down.

God Draws, He Doesn't Shame

I grew up a preacher's kid. Every week was filled with church attendance and activities. This was the time of wearing your Sunday best, so I was expected each time I was at church to put effort into looking nice.

It wasn't lost on me that people paid some attention to what I was doing and how I responded to things. At some point putting my best effort forth just became part of the routine.

Fast-forward to my early 20s, newly married, and having a particularly tough time with my hair one Sunday morning (we were only three years removed from the high-maintenance 80s-hair era).

I remember blurting out in frustration, "I don't even wanna go to church!"

My husband, ever the calm one, simply stated, "Who's making you go? I'm not making you go."

Huh.

I thought about that for a minute, put my brush and can of Aqua Net down, and stayed home. And then I proceeded not to go to church for about six weeks.

To be honest, that first week was such a relief. The pressure to present myself any kind of way for others was mercifully lifted. It felt like playing hooky but there was no one to "catch me."

I was an adult making an adult decision. I thought I was being so grown up. And then around that sixth week, in a quiet moment, I heard Jesus simply ask me, "What will you do with me?"

It wasn't a shame-on-you for not going to church or a demand. It was a simple question.

The longer I sat there, the more I realized how much of my relationship with Him had been clouded by ritual and works for works' sake.

In my haste to get some breathing room from obligation, I had now also pushed aside the One who had given it all to save me. That felt like a weighted blanket across my heart.

"What will you do with me?"

Instead of riding coattail on my family's call, I was now being called. Just me and Him. That was the first moment I remember a relationship with Jesus feeling like a real relationship.

Romans 8:1 says, *"So now there is no condemnation for those who belong to Christ Jesus."*

Jesus coaxed me to examine myself with a pretty great question. And when I saw just how far I'd missed the mark, He was there with forgiveness.

His call is never from shame, just conviction that leads to repentance. And repentance leads to restoration.

Where Have You Been Confusing the Two?

Think about the voices in your head right now. Are they telling you what you did wrong? Or that you *are* wrong Are they pointing to specific actions you can take? Or attacking your identity, especially your identity in Christ?

Guilt says: "You made a mistake. You can fix this."

Shame says: "You are a mistake. You can't be fixed."

So when that voice starts whispering that you're not enough, that you're too broken, that you'll never be useful…

Remember what God says. No more shame. No more disgrace. You will no longer remember the shame of your youth.

That's God's word. And it's final.

***

IN THIS MOMENT

1. **Make a list of things weighing on you right now.** Write down everything making you feel bad: mistakes, failures, regret, areas where you feel like you're not enough.

2. **For each item ask these questions:** 1) Am I feeling bad about something I did or about who I am? 2) Does this include a path to make it right, or does it just feel hopeless 3) Would a loving parent say this to their child, or does it sound cruel? 4) Does this feeling push me toward God or away from Him? Place a "G" (guilt) or "S" (shame) next to each item.

3. **Draw two columns on a new piece of paper.** Label the left column "Guilt (God's voice)" and the right column "Shame (Enemy's voice)." Under guilt, write: "You did something wrong. Here's how to make it right." Under shame, write: "You ARE wrong. There's no fixing you." Transfer your list into the appropriate columns.

4. **Look at the shame column.** These are lies. Cross out each item and write "NOT FROM GOD" over the top of that column. Lay those, along with their powerful feelings, at the

foot of the cross.

5. **For everything in the guilt column, write down one specific action you can take to address it.** Apologize to someone. Make restitution. Change a behavior. Confess it to God and receive forgiveness. Take at least one of these actions today, and thank God for helping you see what will help grow instead of shrink in shame.

***

OTHER MOMENTS

> Those who look to him for help will be radiant with joy; no shadow of shame will darken their faces.
>
> Psalm 34:5

> We do this by keeping our eyes on Jesus, the champion who initiates and perfects our faith. Because of the joy awaiting him, he endured the cross, disregarding its shame. Now he is seated in the place of honor beside God's throne.
>
> Hebrews 12:2

But if we confess our sins to him, he is faithful and just to forgive us our sins and to cleanse us from all wickedness.

1 John 1:9

For the kind of sorrow God wants us to experience leads us away from sin and results in salvation. There's no regret for that kind of sorrow. But worldly sorrow, which lacks repentance, results in spiritual death.

2 Corinthians 7:10

DAY 21: What Anxiety and Depression Steal From You

"Give all your worries and cares to God, for he cares about you."

— 1 Peter 5:7

Anxiety and depression keep you from enjoying your own company.

To sit at a cafe table by yourself and watch people go by completely immersed in their own lives.

To be inspired by an older couple in the corner showing sweet affection for each other. Or give yourself a high five that you missed the kind of train wreck clearly happening at table two.

To overhear part of a nearby conversation and laugh out loud when you tag it inside your own head with, That's what she said!

To linger close to world-class art in a famous museum and share a little of the same ether with an artist long departed.

Anxiety and depression snatch your focus from the elegance, beauty, and creativity that God created for you. They throw you in a hall of mirrors where all you see is endless multiples of yourself with no way out.

They lie and tell you because you're alone you have no value. And that it will always be like this.

The Inward Turn

Anxiety and depression turn you inside your own head. They make you focus on what you're not getting, ruminating on what's not working and what's missing.

Never mind that there's so much happening around you and plenty to be grateful for and laugh about.

You can't see it. Because you're trapped in that hall of mirrors, staring at your own reflection, convinced this is all there is.

The Reality of Anxiety and Depression

Anxiety narrows your focus to perceived threats. Your brain scans constantly for what could go wrong, what you're missing, and what you need to control.

This *hypervigilance* is your nervous system stuck in overdrive, keeping your mind and heart exhausted and unable to rest.

Depression does the opposite but with the same result. It floods you with that *anhedonia* we talked about in Day 9, where you struggle to feel pleasure from things that used to bring you joy. Your brain's reward system is dampened, so nothing feels worth the effort.

Both steal your ability to be present and to notice the beauty around you and to experience life as it's happening.

You're either scanning for danger (anxiety) or convinced nothing matters (depression). Either way, you're not living in the bones of your own life. You're trapped in your head, rehearsing the past or catastrophizing the future.

This is why God's command to "not be anxious" is a rescue. He's calling you out of your head and back into the present moment where He actually is.

God Commands Us Not to Be Anxious

Throughout the Bible, God doesn't just suggest we let go of anxiety. He commands it.

Philippians 4:6-7 says, *"Don't worry about anything; instead, pray about everything. Tell God what you need, and thank him for all he has done. Then you will experience God's peace, which exceeds anything we can understand. His peace will guard your hearts and minds as you live in Christ Jesus."*

Don't worry about anything. That's not a suggestion. It's a directive.

God isn't being harsh, but He knows what anxiety does to you. He knows it steals your focus, your peace, and your ability to see the beauty He's placed around you.

My Grandmother's Answer

My grandmother was in her 90s when we were talking about the time she went through late-stage colon cancer in her mid-70s. She did well with chemotherapy and surgery, and ended up living another 25 years.

I asked her one day, "How did you stare down stage four cancer?"

She said, "Honey, I either believe God's going to take care of me or I don't."

A simple answer that belied her lived reality. My grandmother struggled with anxiety for a lot of her adult life. But by the time she reached her 90s, she already knew most of her life story and what God had already done for her.

And she knew that the best way through was to let God take it.

Leave It With God

You can give it to God and ask Him to take it. But then you have to not take it back. That's the hard part, isn't it?

We pray. We hand it over. We say, "Here you go, God, I can't carry this anymore."

And then five minutes later — or five hours, or five days — we're picking it back up.

We're once again convinced we have to manage it ourselves because what if God doesn't come through?

We slip into fear instead of faith. When we leave it with Him, we have to find ways to make sure we don't keep taking it back.

Start With Small Moments

Enjoying your own company begins in the small moments of noticing what's around you, instead of what's wrong with you. Practice feeling present with no pressure to feel anything else.

Sit with your favorite morning coffee and simply notice with all your other senses what's happening around you. Notice the warmth of the cup in your hands or the way the light hits coming through the window.

Notice someone walking by who looks like they're having a really good day. Let yourself be happy for them instead of resentful.

Anxiety and depression want you to believe this beauty happening around you doesn't exist for you. That you're alone and stuck.

But that's a lie. God created beauty for you to experience, to feel deeply, and to rest in.

And He's asking you to trust Him enough with your emotions to actually experience it. That's a good first crack in those mirrors.

***

IN THIS MOMENT

1. **Identify one thing anxiety or depression has stolen from you.** What used to bring you joy that you can't access anymore? Write it down. Now do that thing for 10 minutes today, even if you don't feel like it. Notice what happens.

2. **Practice being present in your body right now.** Close

your eyes. Take three deep breaths. Name five things you can hear. Open your eyes and name five things you can see. Look for something you haven't noticed before. Take another deep breath and feel your body relax. How does it change your perspective?

3. **Write down your version of my grandmother's answer.** Fill in the blank: "I either believe God _____ or I don't." What do you need to trust Him with? Now read it out loud three times. Your brain needs to hear you say it.

4. **Practice giving it to God and not taking it back.** Set a timer for 10 minutes. Hand your anxiety to God out loud. Name what you're giving Him specifically. Then every time you feel yourself reaching for it again during those 10 minutes, say out loud, "I already gave that to You." Without judging yourself, notice how many times you reach for it. Make this an area of focus this next week.

***

OTHER MOMENTS

Don't be afraid, for I am with you. Don't be discouraged, for I am your God. I will strengthen you and help you. I will hold you up with my victorious right hand.

Isaiah 41:10

Give your burdens to the Lord, and he will take care of you. He will not permit the godly to slip and fall.

Psalm 55:22

I am leaving you with a gift—peace of mind and heart. And the peace I give is a gift the world cannot give. So don't be troubled or afraid.

John 14:27

DAY 22: When God Asks You to Let Go

"But forget all that—it is nothing compared to what I am going to do. For I am about to do something new. See, I have already begun! Do you not see it? I will make a pathway through the wilderness. I will create rivers in the dry wasteland."

— *Isaiah 43:18-19*

The hardest thing to let go of isn't the thing itself. It's what you paid for it.

I bought my son a lighted globe for Christmas one year. I paid $99 for it. That seemed like a lot to me, but he said he was learning about countries at school, and this would really help him.

He used it and learned from it. And eventually it ended up at a garage sale.

Where we sold it for five dollars.

I felt wistful watching it go for five dollars. That didn't feel right after paying $99 for it. But it had served its purpose. Holding onto it just because I'd invested that much would've kept me from making space for something more useful for my son.

That pull to hold on is sunk costs at work.

The belief that staying protects what you've already invested. Really, though, it just keeps you stuck with something that no longer serves you.

The Sunk Cost Trap

Here's what happens: you put time, energy, money, emotion into something. It might be a relationship, a job, or a dream.

You reach a point where you realize it's not working. It's not giving back what you're putting in. And it may even be hurting you.

But you can't walk away because what about everything you've already invested? If you leave now, all that time was wasted, all that effort was for nothing.

So you stay. You keep pouring into something that's already empty and trying to recoup your investment.

Economists call this the *sunk cost fallacy,* the irrational commitment to something based on past investment rather than future value.

It's what keeps a lot of people stuck.

When God Asks You to Let Go

Sometimes God will call you to let go of one thing so He can put another thing in your hand. And it's hard to know when that process is supposed to happen.

You pray. You wait. You try to discern. Is this a season to persevere or a season to release?

What I do know is that God doesn't waste your investments. He just redeems them differently than you expected.

Ecclesiastes 3:6 says there is *"A time to search and a time to quit searching. A time to keep and a time to throw away."*

There's a season for holding on, and there's a season for letting go. The problem is we get stuck trying to recoup our investments before we let go. We want to squeeze out every last drop of return.

But what if the return isn't what you think it is?

Nothing's Ever Wasted

I hear this from clients all the time: "If I leave this relationship, then it's like I've wasted all this time."

It's a hard one because on some level it makes sense. Leaving something you've put your heart and soul in feels like leaving a part of you behind.

But you take something from every relationship and every experience. Whether it's a lesson, a skill, a realization about yourself, or simply the knowledge of what you don't want.

Every experience matters. Nothing's ever wasted.

The investment you made wasn't wasted just because it didn't turn out the way you hoped. You learned from it and you grew. You discovered things about yourself you wouldn't have known otherwise.

That's not waste. That's preparation and wisdom.

And God redeems it all.

The Problem of Holding On

Even if a situation is hurtful, there's something in us that wants to give as many chances as possible to get this thing right. Surely the answer isn't just to walk away after all this time.

What about all the good times? How do you just walk away from the beautiful moments that were forged under all that pressure? How do you leave those beautiful diamonds sitting on a pile of ashes?

Or worse, what if it actually gets better when you leave? Now someone else gets to enjoy the sparkling beauty you helped to create.

It takes incredible courage to leave the scattershot of the familiar and predictable for the unknown expanse of "you can do better."

Staying Costs You

Staying doesn't recover the cost, it just delays what's next.

You won't recover your investment by sticking with it. You already got the value from it. Whatever you were supposed to learn, you learned. Whatever you were supposed to experience, you experienced.

Staying in it now, when God's asking you to let go, isn't protecting your investment. It's preventing your next assignment.

You can't hold the new thing God has for you if your hands are still gripping the old thing.

Luke 5:37-38 says, *"And no one puts new wine into old wineskins. For the new wine would burst the wineskins, spilling the wine and ruining the skins. New wine must be stored in new wineskins."*

You can't contain what God wants to do next in the container you're clinging to now. He's asking you to let go and to trust Him. You'll have to believe that what He has ahead is worth releasing what you're holding.

What Might Letting Go Give Back?

God doesn't ask you to release something without having something better waiting. He's not careless with your heart. He is, however, making space for the new thing He's about to do.

Look again at Isaiah 43:19, *"For I am about to do something new. See, I have already begun! Do you not see it?..."*

Can you perceive that new thing trying to spring up? Or are you so focused on what you've already invested that you can't see what God's preparing?

You Already Have What You Need

The lesson is in the growth, the realization, and the preparation for what's next. It's not wasted just because you're letting it go. This thing may have served its purpose.

Believe that every experience matters and nothing's ever wasted, because He's already working everything together for your good.

***

IN THIS MOMENT

1. **Identify one thing you're holding onto because of what you've invested.** Write it down specifically - the relationship, job, dream, city, or commitment. Now write down how long you've been investing in it and what it's cost you (time, money, emotional energy).

2. **Answer this question:** "Am I staying because it's good for me, or because I'm trying to recoup what I've already spent?" If the answer is the second one, circle it. That's the sunk cost fallacy keeping you stuck. Now list the costs of staying stuck.

3. **Make a "What I Gained" list.** Even if this thing ends, what did you learn? What did you discover about yourself? What skills did you develop? What do you now know you don't want? Write at least three things.

4. **Practice the physical release.** Stand up. Hold your hands in tight fists in front of you. Say out loud: "God, I'm letting go of _____." Now slowly open your hands, palms up. Say: "I trust You have something better." Keep your hands open for 60 seconds. Notice how hard it is not to clench them again. Every time you feel the urge to close them, say: "I'm keeping my hands open for what You have next.

***

OTHER MOMENTS

No, dear brothers and sisters, I have not achieved it, but I focus on this one thing: Forgetting the past and looking forward to what lies ahead, I press on to reach the end of the race and receive the heavenly prize for which God, through Christ Jesus, is calling us.

Philippians 3:13-14

This means that anyone who belongs to Christ has become a new person. The old life is gone; a new life has begun!

2 Corinthians 5:17

Wherever your treasure is, there the desires of your heart will also be.

Matthew 6:21

DAY 23: The Work Happens in the Waiting

"For I am waiting for you, O Lord. You must answer for me, O Lord my God."

— *Psalm 38:15*

There are few things more humbling than waiting on God.

Waiting on Him removes any control you think you have over your timeline.

Waiting shows you trust that He will be right on time.

Waiting makes you lay down your compulsion to try to perform in any kind of way to change your outcome.

Waiting suspends you in that space where you don't yet have your answer, but you have enough faith to believe God's big enough to pull it off.

Wait or Move?

One of the hardest things about waiting is knowing when you're supposed to wait and when you're supposed to move forward.

Is this a season to be still and hang back? Or a season to be bold and take action?

Is God asking me to trust Him in the stillness? Or am I just being passive?

That can be so hard to answer. And I think that's intentional. If waiting were simple, if there were a formula or a clear sign every time, we wouldn't need faith. We'd just need a checklist.

But Proverbs 3:5-6 says, *"Trust in the Lord with all your heart; do not depend on your own understanding. Seek his will in all you do, and he will show you which path to take."*

Seek His will. You won't find it in a formula or a system. You do find it when you stay close enough to hear Him, and submitted enough to obey Him. Waiting requires patience to wait for His timing.

Why Waiting Feels Unbearable

When you're waiting, you're living in ambiguity. You have no idea when, how, or if something will resolve. Your brain hates ambiguity. It's wired to efficiently seek certainty and closure.

This is why waiting on God can feel more unbearable than getting a "no." At least with "no," you have resolution. You can grieve and move on. Waiting suspends you in the unknown, and that can activate anxiety.

Anticipatory stress is your body responding to uncertain future outcomes as if they're happening right now. Your cortisol stays elevated. Your nervous system stays on high alert.

You know this feeling, where you scan constantly for signs: Is this the breakthrough? Is this the answer? Is this finally it? Is this my sign?

We confuse waiting with being passive. Waiting is actually active trust under sustained pressure.

It's choosing to believe God is working even when you can't see progress. It's holding your hands open when everything in you wants to clench them and force an outcome.

It may feel like weakness, but that's some of the hardest spiritual work you'll ever do.

Waiting Doesn't Mean You're on Hold

Sometimes waiting feels like you're stuck, sidelined while everyone else moves forward. Other times, it makes you feel plain useless. If you can submit to it, waiting is where God works things out in you.

Isaiah 40:31 says, *"But those who trust in the Lord will find new strength. They will soar high on wings like eagles. They will run and not grow weary. They will walk and not faint."*

Those who trust in the Lord aren't stuck or stagnant. They're being strengthened and renewed.

The waiting is doing something in you that wouldn't happen if you got what you wanted on your timeline.

God's Timing Isn't Random

A few weeks after I started a new job, one of my colleagues told me they had taken two years to fill my position.

They'd had plenty of good candidates come through, but none of them were quite what they were looking for.

So they opted to keep looking until they found the best fit, even though it meant the work they envisioned for the team stayed on the back burner a little longer.

And when I got there, they all agreed that I was the person they were hoping would fill this position. A perfect alignment at the right time.

Two years before that, I was still knee-deep in another position. And it wasn't a good time for me to leave that position. Even once I decided I was ready to go, it still took me a long time to find another position that fit my needs.

So God's timing had to come together in just the right way for each of us to find each other. We both had to wait and trust the thing that was best for us would come along.

If they had filled that position earlier, I wouldn't have been available. If I had left my previous job earlier, they might not yet have known what they needed.

So we carried on in our respective spaces while we waited.

The Holding Pattern Has Purpose

When a plane is in a holding pattern, it's not lost or forgotten. Air traffic control and the pilot both know where the plane is. It's circling, waiting for clearance to land safely in the right conditions and on a runway that's ready.

That's you right now. You're in a holding pattern, and it feels frustrating. You can see where you want to land and you're ready to get on the ground already.

But God says, "Hold on, not yet."

Psalm 27:14 says, *"Wait patiently for the Lord. Be brave and courageous. Yes, wait patiently for the Lord."*

Sometimes we're waiting for God to change our circumstances when He's actually trying to change us. God hasn't forgotten you or abandoned you. And He certainly hasn't lost track of your situation.

He's working even when it feels like nothing's happening.

The waiting just might be the work.

***

IN THIS MOMENT

1. **Bring the "wait or move?" question to God right now.** Set a timer for 10 minutes. Sit in silence with this question: "God, am I supposed to wait or move forward in [specific situation]?" Write down anything that comes to mind - a word, a phrase, a sense of peace or restlessness. Don't force an answer, just listen.

2. **Make a "Waiting Inventory."** Write down one area where you've been waiting. How long have you been waiting? Now

honestly assess: Am I waiting patiently (trusting God's timing) or anxiously (scanning for signs, trying to force outcomes)? Circle which one is true. If it's the second, that's a growth area.

3. **Create a "What God Might Be Building in Me" list.** During this waiting season, what could He be working on? Patience? Trust? Surrender? Character? Humility? Write at least three things. Now pick one and ask: How would my life be different if I had more of this? Write your answer.

4. **Practice the holding pattern prayer physically.** Stand up and slowly walk in a circle (literally). It might feel silly, but circling breaks the anxiety spiral and pulls you into your body and this moment. As you circle, say out loud: "God, I trust You have me in this holding pattern for a reason. I'm circling, not lost. I'm waiting, not forgotten." Circle three times, saying it each time. Let your body feel what the holding pattern is: movement without arrival, trust without answers.

***

OTHER MOMENTS

> The Lord is good to those who depend on him, to those who search for him. So it is good to wait quietly for salvation from the Lord.
>
> Lamentations 3:25-26

> This vision is for a future time. It describes the end, and it will be fulfilled. If it seems slow in coming, wait patiently, for it will surely take place. It will not be delayed.
>
> Habakkuk 2:3

> As for me, I look to the Lord for help. I wait confidently for God to save me, and my God will certainly hear me.
>
> Micah 7:7

> But if we look forward to something we don't yet have, we must wait patiently and confidently.
>
> Romans 8:25

DAY 24: When God Doesn't Explain Himself

"Trust in the Lord with all your heart; do not depend on your own understanding. Seek his will in all you do, and he will show you which path to take."

— *Proverbs 3:5-6*

Someone walks out of your life with no explanation, and you're left holding all the questions.

Why did this happen? What did I do wrong? What could I have done differently?

You replay every conversation and analyze every interaction. You search their social media for clues to where it all went wrong. If you can just understand why, then you can have closure and move on.

But what if closure never comes?

What if the person who left never explains? What if God never answers your "why"? What then?

Closure is a Myth

Our modern society in all its reasoning and enlightenment has us focused on having an answer to everything. It tells you that you can't move forward until you close this loop currently hanging.

You have to have an explanation. Without it, you're stuck. It all stays open, unfinished, and unresolved. And you can't possibly move on until you know why.

But that's not true. Closure is a lie that keeps you stuck in the past, waiting for a neatly-tied bow that may never come.

Waiting For The Final Loop

I see this constantly with clients, especially in relationships where one person breaks it off via text. Or worse, just ghosts and stops responding entirely.

Just says, "I don't want to do this anymore. Bye." Or nothing at all.

It's deeply hurtful because you don't even get the opportunity to understand what went wrong. Was there something you could have done better? Where were you missing the mark exactly?

The relationship feels like an open loop. How can you accept that it's over when you don't understand why it ended?

So you stay stuck on read, or replaying every text and conversation in your head, scanning for clues.

Here's what I gently tell these clients: You're not owed closure.

That sounds harsh, but it's true. Even though they chose a cowardly way to exit the relationship, they're not obligated to explain themselves.

God will hold them accountable for how they left. But they don't owe you an explanation. Stewing over it and waiting for closure that may never come keeps you frozen in the past.

Worse, it keeps you unable and unwilling to move forward.

Let It Go Without an Answer

So how do you let it go without an answer?

God is sovereign. This means that He makes decisions apart from our feedback or influence, and He doesn't owe us an explanation.

We have to trust that if He doesn't allow us to get the larger meaning or an explanation, then there's a reason for it. And we're not necessarily obligated to know what that is.

This is one of the harder things to tell people who are dealing with terrible tragedies in life. We want to know why something so horrible has happened. What larger process could this possibly be working out in me that explains why this horrible thing is happening?

"Make it make sense" is the common interpretation. These are fair questions, but God's sovereignty means He gets to keep some answers to Himself.

Deuteronomy 29:29 says, *"The Lord our God has secrets known to no one. We are not accountable for them, but we and our children are accountable forever for all that he has revealed to us, so that we may obey all the terms of these instructions."*

We're not accountable for what He hasn't revealed. We're only accountable for what He has.

Choose Your Narrative

Part of creating closure is choosing what story you're going to tell yourself about what happened. You can pick whatever story you need in order to start being the hero in your story again.

When you don't get answers, your brain gets really good at filling in the blanks. And usually, it fills them in with the worst possible story.

"They left because I'm not enough. Because I'm too much. Because something's wrong with me."

All stories where you're the villain. But you can choose a different narrative where you're the hero who dodged a bullet in slow motion.

For example: "Now that I see what kind of person they are, I'm grateful they stepped out of my life. That's definitely not the kind of person I'm looking for."

You might not feel that yet, that's okay. You don't have to feel it for it to be true. You can decide for yourself what this means about you and your future.

If you keep telling yourself the story that their leaving proves you're unlovable, that becomes your reality.

But if you tell yourself the story that their leaving made space for something better, that becomes your reality too.

Either way, you're creating meaning. May as well create meaning that moves you forward, don't you think?

Faith Isn't Having All The Answers

Faith is saying, "I don't know why this happened, God. I don't know what You're doing. But I trust You anyway."

And then you learn to live with the lingering question, and let it go so it stops having so much power over you.

Isaiah 55:8 says, *"'My thoughts are nothing like your thoughts,' says the Lord. 'And my ways are far beyond anything you could imagine.'"*

His ways are higher. His thoughts are higher. You can't comprehend what He's doing, even if He explained it. So you let God help you find the courage to move forward without all the answers.

That's how you find the faith and trust to live with unanswered questions.

***

IN THIS MOMENT

1. **Identify one situation where you're waiting for closure.** Write down the specific question you're demanding an answer to. Now write down how long you've been waiting for this answer. Notice if you're more committed to getting the answer than to moving forward.

2. **Name your fear.** What are you afraid will happen if you don't get closure? Write it down. Then ask: Is this fear about the lack of answer, or about what the lack of answer means about me? Circle which one.

3. **Write the letter you'll never send.** Say everything you need to say to the person who left, the situation that ended, or even to God about the unanswered question. Don't hold back. Write until there's nothing left to say. Then seal it away or throw it out, whatever helps you release it.

4. **Choose the narrative that lets you win.** Write down the worst story you've been telling yourself about why this happened. Now cross it out. Write a new story, one that moves you forward as the hero. Example: "Their leaving made space for something better." Read the new story out loud three times, even if you don't feel it yet.

5. **Create your own closure ritual.** Do something physical to mark the end. Burn the letter (safely). Delete their contact. Change something in your space that reminds you of them. Say out loud: "I don't need their explanation to move forward." Then take one step toward your future: text a friend, sign up for something new, plan something to look forward to.

***

OTHER MOMENTS

Oh, how great are God's riches and wisdom and knowledge! How impossible it is for us to understand his decisions and his ways!

Romans 11:33

Just as you cannot understand the path of the wind or the mystery of a tiny baby growing in its mother's womb, so you cannot understand the activity of God, who does all things.

Ecclesiastes 11:5

I know that you can do anything, and no one can stop you. You asked, "Who is this that questions my wisdom with such ignorance?" It is I—and I was talking about things I knew nothing about, things far too wonderful for me.

Job 42:2-3

Lord, my heart is not proud; my eyes are not haughty. I don't concern myself with matters too great or too awesome for me to grasp. Instead, I have calmed and quieted myself, like a weaned child who no longer cries for its mother's milk. Yes, like a weaned child is my soul within me.

> Psalm 131:1-2

DAY 25: Stop Living in Tomorrow's Disaster

"So don't worry about tomorrow, for tomorrow will bring its own worries. Today's trouble is enough for today."

— *Matthew 6:34*

Much of anxiety is lived in the future. Not in preparation, that's wise. But in worry about things that may never happen.

You tell yourself you're being responsible and covering your bases, but you might actually be *catastrophizing*.

This is where you play prophet and king by predicting the end of the world, then trying to prevent it by insisting you micromanage every little moment.

Catastrophizing propels you into tomorrow's disaster instead of grounding you in today's reality.

Planning vs. Catastrophizing

There's a difference between planning and catastrophizing.

Planning says: "A storm might come. I should get ready to make sure I have what I need."

Catastrophizing says: "A storm is definitely coming. It's going to destroy everything. I have to prevent the destruction by controlling every variable."

Planning is prudent. It acknowledges potential problems and takes reasonable steps to address them.

Catastrophizing is anxiety. It assumes the worst will happen and tries to manage outcomes you can't actually control.

Planning gives you peace of mind. Catastrophizing gives you panic.

If your preparation makes you feel more capable and less anxious, that's planning. If your preparation makes you feel more overwhelmed and anxious, that's catastrophizing.

The Control Trap

You're not catastrophizing because you're pessimistic. You're doing it because you think it gives you control. If you can imagine every possible disaster, then you can prepare for it, right? And if you can prepare for it, maybe you can prevent it.

This is your brain's way of trying to manage uncertainty. Catastrophizing feels like you're doing something productive, but in reality you're just exhausting yourself.

Catastrophizing is merely a misguided attempt at control in situations where you actually have very little control. You can't control whether your boss decides to lay you off. You can't control whether your relationship works out. You can't control whether your kid makes good choices.

But you CAN control how much you worry about it. And worrying feels like doing something.

The problem is, catastrophizing gives you the illusion of control while stealing your peace. And when the actual challenge comes, if it comes at all, you're already depleted from fighting an imaginary version of it.

Real preparation involves taking concrete steps you can actually control. Catastrophizing is just rehearsing pain you might never experience.

Forecasting Fear

Living in Florida teaches you the difference between planning and catastrophizing pretty quickly.

Every May, you start hearing messages about preparing your home and getting your supplies together in case there's a hurricane.

And every May, I have to check myself. Am I calmly making a list and gathering cans of SPAM I'll likely never eat? I like to think I am.

Or am I lying awake at 2am imagining my roof flying off and calculating whether the expensive insurance will pay so we can afford to rebuild? This is also sometimes the scenario running the show.

The messages from the media can be intense predicting disaster before the season even starts. So you have to be a bit more diligent to stay out of the catastrophizing mode.

Good planning is making sure you have enough supplies on hand. You know where your shutters are stored or that they're in good working condition on your windows. You know you have enough fuel for the generator if the power goes out. You have your larger bases covered.

So when a storm is imminent, you're not creating your emergency plan from scratch. You just execute it and fill in the blanks when you know exactly where the storm's headed.

There's still anxiety there because it's a hurricane, after all. But because you've planned and prepared, you can plan for the worst and hope for the best.

You're not trying to control the storm. You're preparing for it. And then trusting that you'll handle whatever comes.

Worry Isn't Preparation

Dutch Holocaust survivor Corrie ten Boom said it perfectly:

"Worrying is carrying tomorrow's load with today's strength—carrying two days at once. It is moving into tomorrow ahead of time. Worrying doesn't empty tomorrow of its sorrow, it empties today of its strength."

That's the trap. You think you're preparing for tomorrow, but you're actually draining yourself today.

And when tomorrow comes, with its actual problems, you have no strength left to handle it.

Tomorrow Will Have Enough Worries of Its Own

Jesus knew this, too. That's why He said in Matthew 6:34, *"So don't worry about tomorrow, for tomorrow will bring its own worries. Today's trouble is enough for today."*

You don't have to carry tomorrow's trouble too. In fact, you can't carry tomorrow's trouble because it doesn't belong to today.

That's what manna in the wilderness taught the Israelites. They couldn't store it up or hoard it for tomorrow.

Exodus 16:4 says, *"Then the Lord said to Moses, 'Look, I'm going to rain down food from heaven for you. Each day the people can go out and pick up as much food as they need for that day...'"*

God gave them enough for today. And tomorrow, He'd give them enough again because God wanted them to trust Him daily, not just once.

Plan, But Don't Worry

If you know a challenge is coming, take reasonable steps to get ready for it. But don't live there emotionally.

Proverbs 27:1 says, *"Don't brag about tomorrow, since you don't know what the day will bring."*

All you can do is trust that God will be with you. That He'll give you what you need when you need it.

He's got tomorrow so you don't have to.

***

IN THIS MOMENT

1. **Name your catastrophe.** Write down one specific thing you're catastrophizing about right now. Don't just write "my job," write the full disaster scenario you're imagining. "I'll get fired, won't be able to pay rent, will have to move in with my parents, will never recover professionally..." Get it all out on paper.

2. **Reality check your catastrophe.** Look at what you wrote. Now ask: What's the actual evidence this will happen? Write that down too. Usually the evidence is thin or nonexistent. This is your brain catastrophizing, not reality reporting.

3. **Play the "What If?" game.** Imagine the worst possible scenario actually happens. Play that movie out all the way to its bitter end. When it's all fallen apart in your imagination, ask yourself: Could I handle that? Not would I like it, but could I survive it? Write your honest answer. Usually the answer is yes, which means you're catastrophizing about something you could actually handle if you had to.

4. **Practice the manna prayer.** Every morning this week, before you check your phone, say out loud: "God, give me what I need for today. Just today. I'm trusting You with tomorrow." Then identify one thing you're grateful for right now, in this present moment.

***

OTHER MOMENTS

Give all your worries and cares to God, for he cares about you.
> 1 Peter 5:7

Can all your worries add a single moment to your life? And if worry can't accomplish a little thing like that, what's the use of worrying over bigger things?
> Luke 12:25-26

You will keep in perfect peace all who trust in you, all whose thoughts are fixed on you!
> Isaiah 26:3

Look here, you who say, "Today or tomorrow we are going to a certain town and will stay there a year. We will do business there and make a profit." How do you know what your life will be like tomorrow? Your life is like the morning fog—it's here a little while, then it's gone. What you ought to say is, "If the Lord wants us to, we will live and do this or that."

James 4:13-15

DAY 26: You Can't Earn What You Already Have

"Make it your goal to live a quiet life, minding your own business and working with your hands, just as we instructed you before. Then people who are not believers will respect the way you live, and you will not need to depend on others."

— 1 Thessalonians 4:11-12

You can't love someone into being whole. And you can't perform your way into someone feeling any kind of way about you.

Yet you keep trying. You put your own needs aside because surely if you just do enough, they'll finally see your value.

They'll finally change and love you back the way you love them. But you can't do someone else's work for them. This pattern usually starts long before you ever tried to help anyone else.

The Math Trap

I still remember the sixth-grade math test that broke me.

In Mrs. Rodriguez's portable classroom with the noisy air conditioner, I stared at long division problems that felt like a foreign language. I'd always struggled with math, but this test was different. It felt impossible.

I looked around the room. Everyone else seemed to be breezing through. The only sound was the tap-tap-tap of pencils on desks.

For the first time, I thought, I'm never going to get this. I'm just not smart enough. I remember what it felt like to let go of the sliver of rope I was still holding onto. Sitting in that desk, I just gave up.

It was the first time I remember letting a skill deficit say something about me as a person.

It felt like equal parts relief at not having to try so hard anymore, and terror at the thought of a future of failing hard. How did I even make that connection between struggling with division and being a failure at life?

That moment has defined me ever since. It's been one of the hardest limiting beliefs to untangle.

This is called the *ease fallacy*. If something's hard, you must not be meant for it. If you're struggling, you're not capable. It's such a trap.

Struggle isn't a sign of failure. It's where your greatest growth happens. But on that day in Ms. Rodriguez's class, I projected my struggle with math onto my intelligence, and let it say something about my worth.

That pattern followed me into adulthood.

In my corporate work, I became convinced perfect performance would finally prove my value. I'd stay late perfecting speeches and presentations, comparing my output to everyone else's.

But no amount of perfect work ever made me feel secure. The bar kept moving. I was never quite good enough because the acceptance I was working so hard for was never about performance in the first place.

This same pattern shows up in relationships.

When Helping Becomes Enabling

In therapy, when clients tell me their greatest weakness is "giving too much," it's a clue there's codependency at play.

Putting your own needs completely aside for another person, even if they're the person you would give your life for, signals a need for validation.

You give hoping people will notice and give you something in return. That doesn't make you a bad person, but it does signal an unmet emotional need that you think can't be met just by being who you are.

The giving is doing something for you. That's a recipe for feeling trapped, exhausted, and resentful because it's based on how well you perform.

And the person you're "helping" doesn't get better, because you're not actually helping them. You're enabling them.

Galatians 6:4-5 says, *"Pay careful attention to your own work, for then you will get the satisfaction of a job well done, and you won't need to compare yourself to anyone else. For we are each responsible for our own conduct."*

You miss out on loving each other fully because you both aren't doing your own work.

The Codependency Pattern

If performance equals worth, then giving equals earning. You meet their needs hoping they'll meet yours. You make yourself useful hoping to become valuable.

This is external validation, basing self-worth on other people's responses instead of your inherent value.

You give from an empty tank, hoping they'll fill it. But they can't. What you're seeking is internal, the belief that you matter just because you exist.

You Can't Do Someone Else's Work

Compassion says, "I see you're struggling. I'll walk with you and support you. But I can't do the work for you."

Codependency says, "Oh, let me fix it for you. If you fail, it says something about me."

Compassion respects boundaries. Codependency takes on responsibility that isn't yours, and keeps the other person from growing.

Proverbs 19:19 says, *"Hot-tempered people must pay the penalty. If you rescue them once, you will have to do it again."*

If you keep rescuing someone from consequences, you're shielding them from the very thing God may be using to grow them. And if you're trying to earn acceptance from people through performance, you're probably doing the same thing with God.

Even with God, We Perform

I did this with God too. If I couldn't earn acceptance through perfect work, maybe I could earn it through perfect faith.

But God doesn't grade on a curve. He's not comparing your prayer life to mine or your service to someone else's.

Romans 5:8 says, *"But God showed his great love for us by sending Christ to die for us while we were still sinners."*

Own Your Own Work

Keep your eyes on your own work. Focus on what God's called you to do, and take care of what He's placed in your hands.

God loves you fully and without performance. That's enough to make you enough.

***

IN THIS MOMENT

1. **Name your "sixth-grade moment."** When did you first learn that performance equals worth? Write down that specific moment or memory. That's the belief driving your codependency today.

2. **Identify one person you might be enabling.** Who are you helping in a way that keeps them from growing? Write their name. Now ask: Am I doing this because they need it, or because I need them to need me? Figure out what you're getting out of it.

3. **List what you're doing for them that they should do themselves.** Write three specific things. Then pick one and make an effort to stop doing it this week. Practice saying to them: "I believe you can handle this yourself."

4. **Rewrite your worth statement.** Write this on a card: "My worth doesn't come from my performance. God loves me fully, without conditions. That's enough." Read it every morning this week before you check your phone.

***

OTHER MOMENTS

Share each other's burdens, and in this way obey the law of Christ... For we are each responsible for our own conduct.

Galatians 6:2, 5

He saved us, not because of the righteous things we had done, but because of his mercy. He washed away our sins, giving us a new birth and new life through the Holy Spirit.

Titus 3:5

Even while we were with you, we gave you this command: "Those unwilling to work will not get to eat.

2 Thessalonians 3:10

God saved you by his grace when you believed. And you can't take credit for this; it is a gift from God. Salvation is not a reward for the good things we have done, so none of us can boast about it.

Ephesians 2:8-9

DAY 27: When God Uses a Donkey

"Then the Lord gave the donkey the ability to speak. 'What have I done to you that deserves your beating me three times?' it asked Balaam."

— Numbers 22:28

This story in Numbers 22-24 is wild.

And I mean that literally. A donkey talks. A pagan con man gets taken over by God. A king's curse gets flipped into a blessing.

The whole thing is a demonstration of God's power and sovereignty in a way He's never shown Israel before. And the lesson is that God will use absolutely anything to accomplish His purposes.

Even a donkey.

The Setup

Israel is camped on the plains of Moab, getting ready to enter the Promised Land. King Balak sees them coming and freaks out. The verse describes it as they "covered the face of the earth," so this crowd was massive.

Balak does what any terrified king would do: he asks for a celebrity psychic to visit him. Balaam is a famous divine seer of the day, a known fortune-teller who makes money telling people what they want to hear. He's a pagan con man with a real reputation.

Balak wants Balaam to curse Israel and use his supposed power to stop them from taking over. But God has some very funny other plans.

God Takes Over

God speaks to Balaam and tells him not to go to Balak and curse Israel because Israel is blessed. God doesn't normally talk to Balaam because he's not a righteous man. But God is sovereign, which means He can use whoever He needs to for His purposes to be fulfilled.

So Balaam complies, but Balak keeps offering him more money. Eventually, God lets Balaam go, but with one condition: "Only say what I tell you to say."

So Balaam saddles up his donkey and heads out to visit the king.

When a Donkey Sees What You Don't

While they're on the journey, God sends an angel to block the path. Balaam can't see the angel, but the donkey clearly can.

You can imagine how terrified an animal would be in seeing an angel. The donkey tries to avoid the angel, which angers Balaam because he thinks the donkey's just being obstinate. So he beats this poor animal.

Three times the angel appears. Three times the donkey tries to avoid it. And three times Balaam beats the donkey for not cooperating. After the third time, the donkey turns around and speaks.

"What have I done to you that deserves your beating me three times?" he says.

You would think this is the part where Balaam says, "Wait, what? A talking donkey?!"

Instead, he just talks right back to it. "You've made me look like a fool!"

God's Humbling Message

The bigger story, apart from Balaam being in some kind of biblical Pixar moment, is that God didn't have enough respect for Balaam to show him the angel directly.

He let the angel appear to the dumbest animal in the caravan first. Then He let that dumb animal correct Balaam and put him on the right path.

Balaam is this famous, powerful, respected figure of supernatural pagan things. And God humbles him by using a donkey to communicate truth about...supernatural things.

God could've used anything. But He chose the lowest, most unlikely messenger to get His point across.

God Uses Whatever He Needs

Balaam shows up to curse Israel. But every time he opens his mouth, God takes over. Instead of curses, blessings come out.

Beautiful, poetic prophecies about Israel's future. Refrains about how God will protect them, that the Messiah will come from Jacob's line.

Balak is furious. He keeps trying to get Balaam to curse Israel. But Balaam simply can't. I picture Balaam speaking these words and then shrugging like, "I don't know what's happening either."

God is speaking through him because God is using him just like He did that donkey: as a tool.

Balaam wasn't chosen or anointed, and he certainly wasn't holy. But God used him just the same.

You Don't Have to Be Special

This story is a demonstration to Israel — and to us — that God is in complete control. We think God needs our best credentials, or a well-developed platform so He can use us to communicate His message with polish and excellence.

God doesn't need any of those, and He doesn't even need us to be of great reputation. He can use a pagan con man and a talking donkey to accomplish His purposes just as easily as He can use a prophet or a king.

And God will use whatever, or whoever, He needs to deliver His message.

God's Sovereignty on Display

God was making the point to Israel that even when their enemies tried to curse them, God controlled the outcome. When a powerful king hired the most famous seer in the region, God was still sovereign.

Before Israel even arrived on the scene, God was already working on their behalf. He turned their enemies' curses into blessings. Their enemies were powerless against them when God's in control of the script.

The story demonstrates that when God is for you, it doesn't matter who's against you.

When You Feel Unqualified

I'm certainly not saying you're a dumb donkey. But I know you might be reading this thinking, "I'm not special enough for God to use me."

God doesn't need your special skills or abilities. He used a donkey, a pagan con man, a stuttering murderer (Moses), a teenage shepherd (David), and a group of uneducated fishermen (the disciples).

He's gotten good results from using the unlikely, the unqualified, and the humble. When He does, there's no question about who gets the glory.

God Works on Your Behalf

The bigger truth in this story is what it shows about God's character. God was working for Israel before they even knew they needed Him to. He turned an enemy's curse into a blessing. He protected them from a threat they didn't even see coming.

And He's doing the same thing for you.

God is working on your behalf in ways you can't see yet. He's turning what was meant to harm you into something that blesses you. He's using unlikely circumstances, unlikely people, and unlikely moments to accomplish His purposes in your life.

All you have to do is trust Him.

***

IN THIS MOMENT

1. **Read Numbers 22-24.** It's quirky and unexpected and shows God's power in a completely unique way. As you read, write down one other thing, besides a talking donkey, that surprises you about how God works in this story.

2. **Write your "unlikely circumstances" story.** Look back at your life. Where has God used unlikely circumstances or unlikely people to accomplish something you needed? Write down the specific story: what you needed, who/what God used, how it turned out. Keep this somewhere you can reread it when you feel unqualified.

3. **Name one area where you feel unqualified right now.** Now ask God: "What if You want to use me here BECAUSE

I feel unqualified? What if my weakness is the point?" Write down whatever comes to mind, even if it's just a whisper.

4. **Pray this:** "God, I don't have to be special for You to use me. You can use anyone and anything. Use me. I'm here. I'm willing." Journal the thoughts that come to your mind.

***

OTHER MOMENTS

Instead, God chose things the world considers foolish in order to shame those who think they are wise. And he chose things that are powerless to shame those who are powerful.

1 Corinthians 1:27

Each time he said, "My grace is all you need. My power works best in weakness." So now I am glad to boast about my weaknesses, so that the power of Christ can work through me.

2 Corinthians 12:9

But the Lord said to Samuel, "Don't judge by his appearance or height, for I have rejected him. The Lord doesn't see things the way you see them. People judge by outward appearance, but the Lord looks at the heart."

1 Samuel 16:7

DAY 28: Carrying Decisions That Aren't Yours

"Then Jesus said, 'Come to me, all of you who are weary and carry heavy burdens, and I will give you rest. Take my yoke upon you. Let me teach you, because I am humble and gentle at heart, and you will find rest for your souls. For my yoke is easy to bear, and the burden I give you is light.'"

— Matthew 11:28-30

You're exhausted by decisions.

What to wear. What to eat. What email to answer first. What to do about your kid's problem. How to fix your coworker's mistake. Whether your spouse should take that job.

Wait. Which of those are actually yours?

You're carrying decisions that don't belong to you. Some belong to other people and others may belong to God.

Why Your Brain Runs Out of Decisions

Every decision depletes your mental energy. It's aptly called ego depletion. Your brain has a finite decision-making capacity each day.

Think of it like a battery. Every choice drains power. By evening, you're dangerously low at 5% and looking for a way to charge up.

But you're not just making YOUR decisions, you're making everyone else's too.

Your kid can't decide what to wear, so you pick their outfit. Your coworker can't decide how to handle a client, so you jump in with a solution. Your spouse is stressed about a job offer, so you throw out some variables to consider.

And every decision that isn't yours drains that battery even faster because you're processing the choice, along with managing the guilt, anxiety, and maybe even resentment.

In Acceptance and Commitment Therapy, we teach *values clarification*. This means knowing your North Star so your decisions align with what matters most. Every decision should pull you toward that North Star.

But even when you have a North Star in Jesus, it's still hard to know sometimes which decisions are actually yours.

How do you know when to help and when you're carrying a burden that isn't yours?

Deciding My Own Future

Years ago when my husband asked about going back to school for my master's in counseling, I couldn't give a clear answer.

Sure, it was my future, my career, and my decision. But I couldn't answer with a resounding yes. My son needed my time. I had a demanding job. And my husband was busy in ministry, which meant I was carrying ministry decisions too with my time.

I was already making so many decisions for other people that I barely had any capacity for my own.

I'd just come out of a job that required what felt like life-or-death decisions every day. Add in mothering, ministry, and everyone else's problems, by the time he asked me that question, my decision battery was at zero.

"I don't know," I said. "I really can't decide right now."

So he stepped in. "Let's at least get you started and see where it goes."

So we drove to the university on my lunch break. By the end of the day, I'd talked to the admissions director and applied, and later, tested and gotten my acceptance letter.

Once I got going with the counseling program, I knew I was in the right place. But I was in a place in my life where I wasn't connecting with what I wanted. And it was making it hard for me to make firm decisions.

I didn't need someone to make the decision for me. But I needed clarity on my values so I could make my own decision. My husband's intervention overrode my decision fatigue and let me at least explore my options.

Moses Carried Everyone's Decisions

Moses had a similar problem.

Exodus 18 says he sat from morning until evening, judging disputes for all of Israel. They brought every problem and every decision to Moses. That sounds pretty exhausting.

The heaviness of that work must have started to show in his personal time because his father-in-law, Jethro, inserted himself into the process with some wise counsel: Teach them how to decide for themselves.

In Exodus 18:22, he says, *"..have them bring the major cases to you. Let the leaders decide the smaller matters themselves. They will help you carry the load, making the task easier for you."*

I'm sure after all they had been through together from slavery in Egypt until now, Moses felt like he had a personal stake in the direction of their lives. But with their large numbers now, it was just too much.

Moses was exhausting himself carrying decisions that belonged to other people. He needed another perspective to help him see where he needed to let people decide for themselves.

What God Actually Wants From You

Moses thought his job was to decide everything for everyone. But Jethro showed him his job was to teach them how to hear from God themselves.

I tell parents of teens struggling to make independent decisions the same thing. When your child asks at a restaurant, "What should I order?" don't answer with your opinion. Instead ask, "What are you thinking about ordering?"

Watch what happens. They start processing out loud.

"Well, they have chicken, which I always order when I'm here. But they also have steak, and I haven't had that in a while..."

They already know how to think it through. They just needed someone to redirect the question back to them so they could tap into their own resources. That's what Jethro did for Moses. And that's what you can do when people bring you their decisions.

When someone brings you a decision, don't decide for them. Ask them these three questions.

- "What are you thinking? Walk me through your options."

- "Which choice requires more faith?"

- "What do you sense God is saying?"

You can do this for everything from what to order for dinner to where to go to college. Most of the time, they already know the answer. They just need someone to help them think it through.

Your job isn't to be their decision-maker. It's to help them become better decision-makers.

When you stop deciding for people and start helping them hear from God themselves, you're no longer carrying decisions that aren't yours.

What's Actually Yours?

Which decisions are you carrying that don't belong to you? Release them. Carrying decisions that aren't yours depletes you from making the ones that are.

Focus on what God placed in your hands and let the rest go.

IN THIS MOMENT

1. **Make three lists.** Title them: "My Decisions," "Shared Decisions," "Their Decisions/God's Decisions." Write down every decision you're currently carrying. Be ruthlessly honest about which column each one belongs in. Most of your exhaustion is in that third column.

2. **Practice the redirect question this week.** Every time someone asks you to make a decision for them, ask, "What are you thinking?" or "Walk me through your options." Don't answer. Just listen. Count how many times you do this by the end of the week. Your goal is to redirect at least three decisions back to the person asking.

3. **Release one decision to God right now.** Write down one outcome you've been trying to control that only God can determine. Read it out loud: "God, this isn't mine to control. I'm giving it to You." When you're tempted to pick it back up this week, remind yourself that it doesn't belong to you.

***

OTHER MOMENTS

"This is not good!" Moses' father-in-law exclaimed. "You're going to wear yourself out—and the people, too. This job is too heavy a burden for you to handle all by yourself... They should always be available to solve the people's common disputes, but have them bring the major cases to you. Let the leaders decide the smaller matters themselves. They will help you carry the load, making the task easier for you."

Exodus 18:17-18, 22

I will come down and talk to you there. I will take some of the Spirit that is upon you, and I will put the Spirit upon them also. They will bear the burden of the people along with you, so you will not have to carry it alone.

Numbers 11:17

A spiritual gift is given to each of us so we can help each other.

1 Corinthians 12:7

> Without wise leadership, a nation falls; there is safety in having many advisers.
>
> Proverbs 11:14

DAY 29: You Can Just Pray Things

"But when you pray, go away by yourself, shut the door behind you, and pray to your Father in private. Then your Father, who sees everything, will reward you. When you pray, don't babble on and on as the Gentiles do. They think their prayers are answered merely by repeating their words again and again. Don't be like them, for your Father knows exactly what you need even before you ask him!"

— Matthew 6:6-8

You don't need fancy words to pray. You don't need to speak language from Shakespeare's day. You don't even need to sound spiritual.

God already knows what you mean and He knows what you need. He already knows what's in your heart.

Your prayers aren't a performance. They're a reach-out to the One who created you who wants to spend time hearing from you.

A Conversation with God

I know many people who've been Christians for years who won't pray out loud. They love God, but they're terrified of how they'll sound.

"What if I use the wrong words? What if I don't sound spiritual enough? What if people think my prayer is shallow?"

This is especially true if you grew up in liturgical churches where prayer was formal, scripted, or reverent. You learned that prayer has a certain sound and cadence.

Or maybe you grew up hearing people pray eloquently, quoting Scripture like Billy Graham, using beautiful, poetic language they seemed to easily pull off the top of their head.

If you think either of those is the standard, you might struggle to pray at all — out loud or silently — because your unpolished prayers might feel inadequate.

But prayer isn't performance art. It's a conversation with God. And unlike your ninth grade English teacher, He's not grading your vocabulary.

What Happens When You Pray

Recent studies show that just 12 minutes of prayer creates neurochemical changes in your brain.

Prayer activates the *prefrontal cortex* (the part of your brain responsible for focus and emotional regulation) and decreases activity in the *parietal lobe* (the part that orients you in space and time).

Your brain literally changes when you pray. Stress hormones decrease, and dopamine and serotonin both go up. The parts of your brain associated with anxiety quiet down. I'm amazed that God built in this neat little benefit to prayer.

So prayer rewires you. It has nothing to do with the right words or how holy you sound. It's your submission to intentionally connect with God.

Jesus knew this. This is why He withdrew from others to pray constantly. He knew prayer was about communing with His father, and how vital that was to what Jesus came to do.

When Prayer Didn't Change Circumstances

The night before Jesus was crucified, He went to the Garden of Gethsemane to pray.

Luke 22:41-44 says He *"...knelt down and prayed, 'Father, if you are willing, please take this cup of suffering away from me. Yet I want your will to be done, not mine.' Then an angel from heaven appeared and strengthened him. He prayed more fervently, and he was in such agony of spirit that his sweat fell to the ground like great drops of blood."*

Jesus was in such agony that He sweat blood. I've prayed some hard prayers, but I don't recall ever praying that hard. Clearly this was a prayer of raw emotion and agony.

"Father, if there's any other way... please."

Even so, God's answer was still the cross. Prayer didn't change His circumstances. But it prepared His heart for what was coming.

After that prayer, Jesus stood up and walked toward His arrest. He surrendered. Prayer had done its work. If Jesus, fully God and fully man, needed to pray like that, what does that say about us?

You Can Just Say Things

So what does an honest prayer actually sound like, then? It sounds like any other conversation you might have with someone you trust.

It's just what's in your heart right now. Don't make it any more complicated than that. Don't overthink the words or how it's coming across. Open your mouth and simply tell God what's going on with you.

He's waiting to meet you.

***

IN THIS MOMENT

1. **Pray for 12 minutes right now using your normal voice.** Set a timer. Talk to God like you'd talk to someone you love - no "prayer voice," or formal language. Just tell Him what's on your mind. Notice what happens in your body and emotions as you do this. Write down how you feel afterward.

2. **Pray like Jesus in Gethsemane about one hard thing.** Choose something you're dreading or afraid of. Pray: "Father, if there's any other way, please... but I want Your will,

not mine." Write down what you're afraid of and what surrendering it to God's will feels like.

3. **Pray out loud with someone this week.** Choose someone safe and tell them that you're practicing praying. Let them hear you talk to God like a friend. Notice your discomfort. That's your performance anxiety. Push through it and notice how it feels.

***

OTHER MOMENTS

In those days when you pray, I will listen.
Jeremiah 29:12

And so I tell you, keep on asking, and you will receive what you ask for. Keep on seeking, and you will find. Keep on knocking, and the door will be opened to you. For everyone who asks, receives. Everyone who seeks, finds. And to everyone who knocks, the door will be opened.
Luke 11:9-10

Always be joyful. Never stop praying. Be thankful in all circumstances, for this is God's will for you who belong to Christ Jesus.

1 Thessalonians 5:16-18

Don't worry about anything; instead, pray about everything. Tell God what you need, and thank him for all he has done.

Philippians 4:6

So let us come boldly to the throne of our gracious God. There we will receive his mercy, and we will find grace to help us when we need it most.

Hebrews 4:16

DAY 30: Standing at the Edge of the Jordan

"Look! He has placed the land in front of you. Go and occupy it as the Lord, the God of your ancestors, has promised you. Don't be afraid! Don't be discouraged!"

— Deuteronomy 1:21

The journey with this book started more than two years ago.

I got the idea as the next installment in my *31 Days* series. My first book, *31 Days of Mental Health Moments*, was a devotional-style book for mental health, so writing an actual devotional book felt like the natural next step.

I wrote the first draft. I designed the cover. I got the idea to make postcards to hand out at a conference I was attending to build early buzz. I even put a QR code on the back. I was eager to share about the book.

And then I chickened out.

I can't even really tell you why except there's a good chance I was afraid I wouldn't be able to produce a book that would live up to the weight of the topic.

Scripture is important to me. I never want it to feel thrown together or touched on lightly. It deserves to be handled with care and reverence.

But Jeremiah 29:11 has also been top of mind: *"'For I know the plans I have for you,' declares the Lord. 'Plans to prosper you and not to harm you, plans to give you hope and a future.'"*

That verse makes me think the ideas I have do come from God. He gives me what I need to know in pretty clear detail and actionable instructions.

But I'm the one not taking them into the Promised Land. Instead, I prefer to wring my hands and wonder why God brought me here to wander around in the wilderness.

God showed me the opening scripture in this chapter just this morning. It reads like a victorious declaration, doesn't it?

Deuteronomy 1:21: *"Look! He has placed the land in front of you. Go and occupy it as the Lord, the God of your ancestors, has promised you. Don't be afraid! Don't be discouraged!"*

This is Moses' address to the Israelites as they stood just over the Jordan River. You would think he was giving them a pep talk before they finally cross over the river into God's purpose for them.

But he's actually delivering a farewell address, where he's sort of recapping previous seasons of *The Exodus Tales*. Moses already knows he won't be entering the Promised Land due to his own disobedience. So he's giving this new generation some history before he's no longer in the picture.

A lot has happened in forty years, but not the main directive God had given His people right at the start: Journey to the Promised Land and take it. Yes, I know that sounds scary, but don't worry, I'm with you.

Now, a generation later, this verse isn't aimed at the Israelites as they stand ready to cross over. Moses isn't trying to get them fired up. He's walking them down memory lane, reminding them that God gave them this promise right out of Egypt.

When they left Egypt, they were only eleven travel days from the Promised Land. But because of their fear, rebellion, and discouragement, they spent 40 years complaining about their circumstances and piddling around in the wilderness looking lost.

They had delayed His promises by doing the very thing He commanded them not to in that verse: being afraid and discouraged.

Even so, over those forty years, God still met their needs in the wilderness and gave them innumerable chances to get back on track. Now Moses is reminding them they are back at that same place, poised in front of the land God promised them once more, to do what He had set out for them from the beginning.

When I saw that scripture this morning, I felt convicted. How long ago did God give me the parts of the plan I needed to know? But I was also excited.

I felt like God was returning me to the original plan He gave me from the get-go. The land is in front of me again.

And as I sit here late at night, alone in my tiny office, tired and dry-eyed, pushing against this wall trying to push me away from publishing this thing, I realize I'm at risk of doing exactly what kept me in the wilderness two years ago.

I'm listening to the voice of fear.

Two years ago, I felt God give me the momentum to bring this work forward. But I listened instead to the voice that said, "How will YOU make this good enough."

You're too close to the edge. You don't have enough time. It's too wordy. It's too bland. It doesn't read like a Sarah Young or an Oswald Chambers devotion. It doesn't even read like its own impassioned opening section, "The Greatest Love Story Ever Told."

Look at me telling God what will speak to people and what won't, about a book He asked me to write. Face palm.

I don't know who needs this book.

I don't know who's struggling to build a daily habit of time with God and this book gives them an easy thing to return to for 31 days.

I don't know who's been wandering in the wilderness, thinking they're doing things for God, but delaying what He actually asked them to do.

What is it in me that needs to qualify this and not trust that God has brought me to this intersection right now?

Remember Esther? She could have just enjoyed where she was, safe, comfortable, luxurious queen of Persia enjoying endless spa days.

But Mordecai reminded her in Esther 4:14, *"If you keep quiet at a time like this, deliverance and relief for the Jews will arise from some other place, but you and your relatives will die. Who knows if perhaps you were made queen for just such a time as this?"*

She had to do the work God had prepared her to do. Even if it cost her her life.

"If I must die, I must die," she said in Esther 4:16. But she didn't die. She kept her trust in God and saved her people.

Maybe that's where I am now. Maybe that's where you are, too, when you're reading this in the future. Standing at the edge of something God prepared you for but, unlike Esther, afraid to step in.

So here's what I'm asking myself, and what I'm asking you:

What Promised Land are you standing in front of right now? What has God been calling you to do that you've been delaying because of fear? What idea, what step of obedience have you been circling in the wilderness instead of crossing the Jordan?

God will meet your needs in the wilderness. He always has. But He has something better waiting for you on the other side of obedience.

Deuteronomy 1:21 says it again, *"Do not be afraid; do not be discouraged."*

The land is in front of you. God has already given it to you. He gave it to you when He gave you your hope and your future. All you have to do is go.

Maybe the timing wasn't right for this book two years ago. But at some point, I have to trust God with what He's given me and let Him do the work that must be done with it.

I'm publishing this book tomorrow. I'm crossing my Jordan.

What's yours?

***

IN THIS MOMENT

1. **Identify your Promised Land.** What has God been calling you to do that you've been delaying? Write it down. Be specific. This is your Jordan River moment.

2. **Name your fear.** What voice is telling you not to go? "Not good enough"? "Not the right time"? "What if I fail"? Write down exactly what fear is saying. Then write Deuteronomy 1:21 over it: "Do not be afraid; do not be discouraged."

3. **Count the cost of delay.** How long have you been circling this? Months? Years? Write down what delaying obedience has cost you. Now write down what crossing the Jordan could give you - not just for you, but for the people God wants to reach through you.

4. **Take one step toward the Jordan this week.** Not the whole journey. Just one step. Make the phone call. Send the email. Have the conversation. Write the first page. Whatever your "one step" is - do it. Then write down how it felt to finally move.

5. **Pray Esther's prayer.** Say out loud: "God, if You've brought me to this moment for such a time as this, give me the courage to step in. If I perish, I perish. But I will not let fear keep me from what You've called me to do." Write down what happens in your heart when you pray that.

***

OTHER MOMENTS

For God has not given us a spirit of fear and timidity, but of power, love, and self-discipline.

2 Timothy 1:7

And if the Lord is pleased with us, he will bring us safely into that land and give it to us... don't be afraid of the people of the land... the Lord is with us! Don't be afraid of them!

Numbers 14:8-9

And I am certain that God, who began the good work within you, will continue his work until it is finally finished on the day when Christ Jesus returns.

Philippians 1:6

DAY 31: The Day Everything Finally Makes Sense

"They sang, 'Amen! Blessing and glory and wisdom and thanksgiving and honor and power and strength belong to our God forever and ever! Amen.'"

— *Revelation 7:12*

Picture the worst season of your life finally ending.

The loss, the betrayal, the sickness, the shame, whatever your personal hell was. You thought you'd never feel safe or clean or whole again.

Now imagine walking into the biggest celebration you've ever seen. Every nation represented, every language spoken, every kind of person present.

They're wearing white, not because they were perfect or holy, but because someone else paid to make them clean.

And they're screaming in pure joy. The One who rescued them is right there in front of them. That's when the angels lose it.

They fall on their faces and shout this seven-word explosion of praise: *"Blessing! Glory! Wisdom! Thanksgiving! Honor! Power! Strength!"*

Every tear, every doubt you had at 2 a.m., every time you thought, "There's no way God can fix this." All of it was leading here.

And you're in that crowd. Your seat's already saved, and the angels are cheering for you too.

This Is How The Love Story Ends

I've put this chapter at the end because it marks the end of the story. Except it isn't the end. It's just getting started.

From the garden where God walked with Adam and Eve. To Jesus who came in the flesh to make a way back. To this, the new heaven and new earth where we're fully restored to Him.

This is the celebration that we are finally, after all this time and struggle, in the presence of God. And it illustrates the majesty of the God we serve while we're on this earth.

Every Promise God Made Comes True

Think about all the promises we've leaned on in these 31 days:

He promised to be our refuge. And He was.

He promised He hadn't forgotten us. And He didn't.

He promised rest from our striving. And He gave it.

He promised to be close even when we couldn't feel Him. And He was.

He promised to guide us when we didn't know whether to wait or move. And He did.

He promised His yoke would be easy and His burden light. And it was, when we stopped striving and started trusting.

Every single promise kept.

And on that day, the day of Revelation 7:12, we'll see it. We'll stand in the middle of it. We'll experience the fullness of every promise He ever made.

All the Little Things Add Up

We're celebrating 31 days of being in God's Word at the beginning of your day.

Every morning you chose to open this book instead of scrolling your phone.

Every moment you paused to ask God for help instead of white-knuckling your way through.

Every time you took your anxious thoughts captive.

Every time you let go of what didn't belong to you.

Every time you gave tomorrow's problems back to tomorrow.

Every time you prayed without performing. Every time you trusted God with the waiting.

Every time you crossed the Jordan instead of listening to fear.

All of it added up.

Not because you did any of it perfectly, but because you tried and you trusted. And God met you there every day.

This Day Will Be the Most Amazing Day Ever

Because of what Jesus did, you can enter this ultimate celebration as someone who's already been made victorious.

In that moment:

- Every struggle you faced in these 31 days? Gone.

- Every tear you cried? Wiped away.

- Every question you asked? Answered.

Because God keeps His promises, and this is the ultimate one.

You're Already Part of the Story

Your seat at the celebration is already saved. The angels are already cheering for you because of what Jesus did for you.

So live and trust Him like you know that.

Because one day — maybe sooner than you think — you'll walk into that celebration. And every hard moment will have been worth it.

But Maybe You're Not Sure Yet

If you've read these 31 days and you're thinking, I want this. I want to be part of this celebration. But I've never actually asked Jesus into my life, today's your day.

Romans 10:9 says, *"If you openly declare that Jesus is Lord and believe in your heart that God raised him from the dead, you will be saved."*

You don't have to clean yourself up first. You don't have to get your act together. You don't have to earn it in any way.

Jesus already paid for your seat at the celebration. You just have to accept it.

If you want to do that right now, pray this with me:

God, I believe Jesus is Your Son. I believe He died on the cross to pay for my sin and rose from the dead. I'm done trying to do this on my own. I'm asking You to forgive me, to save me, to make me Yours. I want to be part of Your story. I want to walk with You. Thank You for loving me. Thank You for making a way. Amen.

If you just prayed that, welcome home! Your seat at the celebration is official now.

Do you hear the angels cheering?

***

IN THIS MOMENT

1. **Look back over these 31 days.** Which day impacted you most? Which truth do you need to carry forward and con-

tinue to work on?

2. **Write down one way God showed up** for you during these 31 days. Describe one moment He was faithful.

3. **Read Revelation 7:9-17.** Let yourself imagine that celebration. You're in it. Your seat is saved. How does that change how you live today?

4. **If you prayed the salvation prayer, tell someone this week.** Text a Christian friend, call a family member, or email a pastor. Let them know you just gave your life to Jesus. Your confession of your faith in Him allows people to celebrate with you and walk with you.

***

OTHER MOMENTS

> I heard a loud shout from the throne, saying, "Look, God's home is now among his people! He will live with them, and they will be his people. God himself will be with them. He will wipe every tear from their eyes, and there will be no more death or sorrow or crying or pain. All these things are gone forever."
>
> Revelation 21:3-4

That is what the Scriptures mean when they say, "No eye has seen, no ear has heard, and no mind has imagined what God has prepared for those who love him."

1 Corinthians 2:9

For our present troubles are small and won't last very long. Yet they produce for us a glory that vastly outweighs them and will last forever! So we don't look at the troubles we can see now; rather, we fix our gaze on things that cannot be seen. For the things we see now will soon be gone, but the things we cannot see will last forever.

2 Corinthians 4:17-18

But we are citizens of heaven, where the Lord Jesus Christ lives. And we are eagerly waiting for him to return as our Savior. He will take our weak mortal bodies and change them into glorious bodies like his own, using the same power with which he will bring everything under his control.

Philippians 3:20-21

Day 32 and Beyond

You did it!

Thirty-one days of showing up, opening God's Word, and building faith one moment at a time.

Maybe some days felt transformative. Maybe others felt like you were just going through the motions. Both count.

Faithfulness isn't measured by how inspired you feel. It's measured by whether you showed up and the condition of your heart when you do.

The real question isn't whether these 31 days changed you. The question is: what happens now?

This book was never meant to be a one-time experience. It was meant to be a tiny foundation.

A starting place.

So keep going.

Pick a Psalm. Read a chapter of Proverbs that matches the day of the month. Work through the Gospels one passage at a time. Or simply start this book again and see what God shows you the second time through.

If you don't already have a Bible, get one. A physical copy you can hold, mark up, and return to.

Or download the YouVersion Bible app (youversion.com). It's free and includes reading plans that guide you through scripture in manageable sections.

The Bible Project (bibleproject.com) is also an excellent resource, especially if you're encountering these stories for the first time. Their videos and guides help make sense of the bigger narrative.

And if you prayed to invite Jesus into your heart while reading this book, there's something else you need to know:

You weren't meant to walk this out alone.

Faith grows in community. Find a local church, a place where you can be known, where you can ask questions, where people will walk with you through both the celebrations and the hard seasons.

Church isn't about being perfect or having it all figured out. Don't let that keep you from going.

It's about showing up, learning together, and being shaped by others who are also following Jesus.

Discipleship matters. Find people further along in their faith who can mentor you. The best way to get started is to join a small group or Bible study.

Surround yourself with others who will encourage you, challenge you, and remind you of the truth when life gets overwhelming.

You've proven you can do this. Now keep building.

And know, that I'm over here cheering for you!

Small Group Resources

Take This 31-Day Journey With Your Small Group

Faith in God grows deeper in connection with others. If this book has challenged or encouraged you, consider inviting your small group, Bible study, or friends to experience it together.

I've created a free 4-week small group discussion guide to help you facilitate meaningful conversations around the themes in this book.

Each week focuses on the days that resonated with your group, with discussion questions designed to move beyond surface-level sharing into real spiritual work.

Download your free guide at:
lorimiller.me/smallgroup

Whether you're leading an established group at your church or gathering friends around your kitchen table, this guide will help you create space for conversation that grow your faith, nurture your mental health, and provide support to choose belief when it's hard.

You don't need to be a Bible study expert. You just need to show up and be willing to wrestle with what it means to live and walk closer with God.

A Request

If this book helped you build your faith, would you consider leaving a review?

Reviews help other readers discover these faith-building moments. Whether you leave a few sentences or a detailed reflection, your honest feedback makes a difference.

You can leave a review on Amazon, Goodreads, or wherever you purchased this book.

Your time is your most valuable asset. I appreciate you using some of it to read this book.

And thank you for helping others find their way to these pages!

About Lori

Lori R. Miller, LMHC is a licensed mental health counselor, author, and speaker who spent twenty years in corporate communications before answering a call to help people rewrite their stories.

With a master's degree in counseling and two decades of experience navigating the complexities of high-pressure corporate environments, Lori brings both professional insight and hard-won personal wisdom to her work.

She understands what it's like to achieve success and still wonder if you're enough.

31 DAYS OF FAITH-BUILDING MOMENTS

Her counseling practice focuses on helping professionals, families, and individuals navigate anxiety, perfectionism, and the exhausting pressure to perform.

For more than 25 years, Lori has served in church ministry alongside her husband, who has held pastoral roles in various churches. Together, they've led youth groups, mentored students, and developed curriculum that helps people discover God's calling on their lives.

This deep foundation in ministry shapes her counseling approach, her writing, and her understanding that spiritual health and mental health are deeply integrated.

Lori also is the author of *31 Days of Mental Health Moments* and is currently working on *Letters to a Smart Girl*, a book for intelligent, accomplished women who want to understand God's unique purpose for their lives.

For more content that bridges faith, audacious belief, and mental health, sign up for Lori's newsletter at **lorimiller.me/subscribe.**

Also by Lori Miller

31 Days of Mental Health Moments

Mental health isn't something you "fix" once and move on. It's something you tend to daily, intentionally, with small practices that add up over time.

31 Days of Mental Health Moments offers bite-sized, practical guidance for managing anxiety, setting boundaries, challenging negative thought patterns, and building emotional resilience.

Each entry is designed to be read in minutes but applied throughout the day.

Whether you're navigating a difficult season, supporting someone who is, or simply want to strengthen your mental and emotional well-being, this book provides accessible, actionable tools grounded in both clinical insight and real-world experience.

Visit **lorimiller.me/books** to get your copy today!

Connect With Lori

Newsletter: Join for regular insights on faith, mental health, and audacious belief: **lorimiller.me/subscribe**

Website: Essays, resources, and all my books: **lorimiller.me**

Speaking: Available for engagements, workshops, and collaboration: **lorimiller.me/contact**

www.ingramcontent.com/pod-product-compliance
Lightning Source LLC
Chambersburg PA
CBHW071956070526
44583CB00015B/1217